THE DEFINITIVE ANSWER TO THE WAR ON DRUGS

By

MICAH CHARLES

authorHOUSE™

1663 LIBERTY DRIVE, SUITE 200
BLOOMINGTON, INDIANA 47403
(800) 839-8640
WWW.AUTHORHOUSE.COM

First published by AuthorHouse 07/11/05

ISBN: 1-4208-6958-2 (sc)

Library of Congress Control Number: 2005905880

Printed in the United States of America
Bloomington, Indiana

This book is printed on acid-free paper.

CONTENTS

PREFACE

I was raised in a middle-class family, the younger of two boys born to Christian conservative parents in a moderate sized suburban city in America. I started taking drugs when I was 13, just two years after I graduated from the D.A.R.E. program at school. I really don't know why I started doing drugs in the first place but it was a very natural transition going from someone who has never even thought about doing drugs, to someone who just did them for the first time. Before I started doing drugs I remember quite clearly the vivid impressions I had of them being these nasty, chemical substances that involved needles, powders, pills, some weird type of acid, and so forth. Marijuana, I was told, was this evil smoke that was 1,000 times worse than cigarettes and that's really all I knew about it. So indeed it was a surprise to find out that Marijuana was just a plant. And when I first saw some Marijuana up close that a friend had, it looked rather harmless, just an herb in its natural form. It wasn't manmade or chemically processed, in fact it looked like some of the herbs I'd seen everyday in my mother's spice rack. It wasn't a powder you snort or a poison you inject, neither was it a processed pill or the strange, ambiguous acid I thought was some type of battery acid. Nope, it was just an honest to God, Mother Nature produced herb that you smoke, and since by then I had smoked tobacco a few times, I was already accustomed to smoking as a method of ingestion. I mean as a kid you see adults doing it everyday. So I began smoking pot, and the high didn't resemble anything like what I was taught in school, it was uplifting, unique, fun, and somewhat enlightening. I didn't have the severe, spiraling crash I was promised in school once the high was over, so I got a little hungry afterwards so what!

I wondered to myself at that young age, how could the people who taught me how bad drugs were, get Marijuana so wrong? Had they even tried it? Cause I knew that if they had, they wouldn't so easily be able to describe it. And surely they wouldn't use such negative words in persuading others of its effects. So right then I learned that you couldn't really believe peoples' opinion on drugs, especially when they have never even done the drug themselves that they're preaching about. That philosophy of experience over opinion shaped the next ten years of drug use for me.

I can admit that I haven't always used drugs in the wisest of ways, but through my experience I have put myself in the unique position of being able to honestly and accurately advise others about drugs, for it is no longer just opinion or here say, it is in-depth, real-world experience. Something that all drug lawmakers lack, something that all D.A.R.E. officers are deficient in, and it's a quality that keeps most research institutes from knowing what path to direct their drug studies towards. And since government agencies do not have any real and personal experience with drugs, they do not know how to form laws governing these substances. For them to try is like having a toddler build your computer, it obviously won't work. But that is the reality of our modern day drug laws. They are old, rigid and were devised from a reaction to what the government perceived drug use was. Never mind being objective or going to the source to learn why people do drugs in the first place, they just stood back from afar and passed laws that in their mind would squash all drugs and drug offenders. On top of that, they embarked on a massive campaign to miseducate people about drugs, their effects, and the harm that arises. They conducted biased research to substantiate their claims while denying approval for independent research organizations to conduct their own studies, and they made no distinction between drugs of greater harm and drugs of no harm or very little harm. The government just grouped them all together under one demonized category of drugs, called them all evil, and of no religious or medical value and set about passing laws and inflicting punishments that were more detrimental to the drug user then the drug itself.

Were they right to do so, did they have justification? Sure drugs that effect human consciousness and bring about temporary mental and physical changes in its users are scary. After all, the government is just protecting society from having a bunch of hopped-up crazies running around everywhere right, while also keeping the people who lack the judgment to abstain, from harming their bodies with these dangerous drugs. And for that we can thank the government, but I also say no thanks to the inflexibility, the excessive penalties, the falsified propaganda, the depriving of medical benefits and the stubbornness to reexamine its stance on certain drugs. No thanks to the wasted money spent prosecuting people for petty possession crimes, and keeping them in prison for non-violent drug offenses. No thanks to a policy that cannot grow, change or adapt. Such a policy is not in the best interest of the people.

There is a lot of money tied up in the Drug War and a lot of injustices also. Some drugs deserve their label of being addictive and dangerous, while others should be freely distributed and celebrated as religious sacraments, recreational endeavors, and medical, miracle drugs. Likewise some drug doers deserve their penalties for their crimes, and should not be allowed to profit from dangerous drugs. But we need to be realistic, denying the existence of a whole culture worldwide and making criminals out of all of them is not going to make drug use go away. It is only going to eat up government resources and put people through unnecessary persecution. And in this world where there is already an enormous amount of human suffering and a substantial lack of government resources, we should not maintain an ineffective policy towards drugs but seek to ease and solve this complex issue of drug use.

My personal experience with drugs has taught me a lot about the substances themselves. I have had very good times and extremely bad times with them. I have used them recreationally and spiritually as well as abused them beyond belief. I know which of these substances are beneficial and lead to positive experiences, and which ones are prone to a constant cycle of degradation. It took me over a decade of examining these drugs inside and out, before I truly knew them well enough to advise others about them. I have witnessed the consequences of the drug law and its effects on the drug abuser. Does it help them recover, teach them and get their life back on track? Or does it keep them in the downward spiral never allowing them to gain ground and progress. With the knowledge I have gained, I can now from experience and not opinion, propose adequate laws of a rational nature and help give answers to the never-ending question that is the Drug War.

INTRODUCTION

We are all aware of drugs and the battle that is taking place to control them. The goal of that battle is to make drugs extinct. Is it going to happen? How close are we in the almost 100 years of drug prohibition? There are still plenty of drugs, plenty of drug dealers and plenty of drug users, there has never even been a dent in the supply of drugs and they are only getting more plentiful and cheaper. Is this a failure we want to continue to dump billions of dollars into every year, while in the meantime our schools go drastically under funded, our poor and elderly receive very little help if any at all, our roads, parks, military, and public services are all under funded, and that's only a few. Every single facet of our society that the government is responsible for overseeing is feeling the squeeze financially. The only way to increase government funds in the past has been one of two options, raise taxes or increase the national deficit. It is a vicious cycle that has yet to see an end. Could a change in the War on Drugs actually help society and reverse this trend? Even if it could, does this mean that we all have to live with a bunch of free-roaming junkies everywhere? No it doesn't, but preventing that from happening while also making the appropriate changes to the War on Drugs is the key solution. Let's look at the current options. There are people and organizations that want to legalize just Marijuana, that's a good idea and it will help a lot especially if it is commercialized and taxed. But the Drug War problem is created from the underground distribution of all drugs. Therefore legalizing just Marijuana will have only a small effect because you still have all the other more profitable drugs to fight. The crime and violence attributed with their distribution will not end, making it necessary to continue spending enormous sums of money and resources combating the Drug War. Another option is to substantially decriminalize all drugs, but then you still have drug distribution and drug-related violence and crime, plus the profitable underground drug market would still exist. And however petty the punishment may be it'll still eat up resources and not solve the overall problem. Some have suggested legalizing all drugs but then require a prescription to obtain them. But even if we do that there will still be an underground network of drug distribution without prescriptions similar to what we have today. If you were to make all drugs legal without a prescription then there would be no control, no limits, free reign on harmful drugs, and drug dealer's still profiting. So it seems like the only solution to end the Drug War is to legalize all drugs but have them commercialized and regulated? That would definitely cut down on the crime and violence attributed to the underground market and bring in a lot of money from taxes. But do we really want substances like Heroin, Cocaine, Crack and Crystal Meth for sale in every community everywhere? Definitely not, and ultimately that solution may solve the Drug War but it perpetuates the drug problem by increasing the availability of dangerous drugs. Trying to devise the answer for the War on Drugs is frustrating isn't it?

My solution is simple, give back to mankind their right to all plants and the Drug War will dissolve itself.

That may or may not make sense to you depending on how familiar you are with drugs, but it is my goal and the labor of this book to educate you on how that statement will lead to the eventual end of the Drug War. This book is broken down into different chapters each of which tackles a different issue concerning drugs, the Drug War, the drug user and legalization. Collectively it will address every concern and question you may have about which drugs we legalize, how we legalize them, how we set up safe guards to prevent abuse, what happens if abuse arises and what to do with the offenders. You will also gain a unique perspective into why people take drugs and how come some users turn into junkies and abuse drugs, while others just simply partake every once in a while for relaxation, medicinal or celebratory purposes.

Solving the Drug War is imperative because it is one of the largest burdens of modern mankind that can easily be fixed with a small change in legislation. It is a burden that single-handedly diverts massive amounts of funds and attention from matters that desperately need those funds and attention more. Plus it persecutes the offending person far more than what should be acceptable under cruel and unusual punishment. It's just that small change in legislation that could fix the Drug War and set it on a path of redemption that will change it from being one of the most inefficient and reckless wastes of money, to a humane and responsible policy that protects people but also gives them back the right to their body and what they choose to put in it. At the same time this new policy on drugs will free up enormous amounts of money already being spent waging the War on Drugs, as well as bring in an entire new source of income from taxes. Taxes? Yes, but don't assume my plan involves selling drugs to junkies, it just isn't that bleak. It's much more involved and logical then that, not to mention humane. With all this new income, the government can then flood other neglected public programs with money that it previously had to scale back on. To even imagine a public education system that has no major budget restraints in today's world is unthinkable, but the possibilities are unlimited in a society not bogged down by unrealistic ideals concerning drug prohibition.

You already know that there are major, fundamental problems concerning the execution of the War on Drugs and you have daunting perceptions about drug use in general. You want to see change but not just change without purpose and direction. You want to see improvement that leads to fewer people abusing drugs, a decreased availability of dangerous drugs, and a free and safe society living side by side with drugs because as we all know they will never go away. The ideas expressed in each chapter will build your knowledge point by point so that you may have a complete understanding of the drug philosophy I have devised. But keep in mind that this is not just another book about the Drug War. You will find no statistics regarding drugs, the Drug War and drug use within these pages. It is not another attempt at regurgitating the struggles and failures of the Drug War, it is in fact the exact opposite. I have written this book with one assumption in mind, and it is that you already know how unsuccessful the War on Drugs truly is. If you didn't then you wouldn't be here looking for the answer.

For those who are unaware of what a cosmic failure the Drug War is, then I suggest that you first read any of the number of books that are just filled with statistics detailing how many hundreds of billions of dollars the war costs every year, and how many addicts get put in jail instead of rehab, just to get released later to abuse the same drugs again. Learn how these non-violent drug offenders overload our jails. Find out first hand if our current drug education is really effective by visiting the neighborhoods that are completely overwhelmed by drug use and drug related crime. Read about how the drug cartels are so powerful in some countries that they are actually fighting their local government for control of the country. And when you hear the government reports on how many millions of pounds of drugs they confiscate every year, be sure to check out the other reports that state how we still only manage to stop less than one-third of all drugs that enter our country. When you understand all that and are fed up with all the other seemingly worthless solutions to the War on Drugs, then read this book and you will understand exactly what it is really going to take to end the Drug War.

Before we get into any specifics of my new drug plan, it is important that you comprehend a certain amount of drug-related knowledge. Therefore the first four chapters are dedicated to ensuring that you know what drugs are and how they are different from each other, and how the Drug War conflicts with some of our basic human rights. It is also equally important that you gain a full understanding of Drug War related concepts and why people choose to get high in the first place. It is only after these foundations are in place that you will be fully equipped to comprehend the new drug philosophy I have devised.

Chapter 01: Plants And Drugs

The first step is to lay the groundwork for your new understanding of drugs. It is important to have some fundamental knowledge about drugs and drug use so that you'll better understand the foundations of this newly presented drug philosophy. This chapter is pretty intensive and contains a lot of concentrated drug information and it may be difficult to retain all this information at first, especially if you previously did not have any drug knowledge. But you should be able to grasp the basics of each drug, if you don't at first then continue reading and you can always come back to this chapter to reacquaint yourself with a certain illegal substance when it is mentioned later.

We need to separate illegal drugs into two categories, the categories being Plants and Drugs. The vast majority of drugs come from plants, they either are plants themselves or are chemicals extracted from plants and then combined with other chemicals. Sometimes they can be just a mix of several synthetic chemicals. Unfortunately today, the law states that illegal drugs are illegal whether they are unchanged plants in their natural form, plant extracts that are chemically processed, or synthetic chemical concoctions. There is no distinction between the different types of illegal substances and so grouping them together under one category called drugs and banning them all outright is what does the real harm. You'll see that there is a huge distinction that divides what are commonly known as illegal drugs. To make this distinction apparent we will have to examine every drug, and define exactly what differentiates it from being either a plant or a drug. First we'll look at the two categories in more depth.

An illegal drug that is actually an unchanged plant is more accurately described as a Psychotropic Plant, also known as entheogens or psychedelic vegetables. They really are any naturally growing fungus or plant or parts of plants including fruits, flowers, leaves or seeds that when consumed by humans, result in temporary changes in perception, consciousness, mood or feeling. They are completely natural growing plants that undergo zero refining in order to produce the before mentioned effects in humans. Some examples of these psychotropic plants are the Marijuana Plant, Psilocybe Mushrooms, the Opium Poppy Flower, the Coca Plant, and the Peyote Cactus. There are hundreds of plants that are psychotropic but the government has only made the most common and profound ones illegal. These plants have been around longer than recorded history and their use dates back to the earliest civilizations of mankind. They are all relatively non-addictive except for the Opium Poppy, which if abused can lead to a dependency, but the addiction provability of Opium is much less than its synthetic representation Heroin. These psychotropic plants have vast amounts of recorded historical and religious use. Every single one of these plants has immense spiritual and enlightenment possibilities and traditionally has been used for such reasons. Their potential to ease human suffering surpasses anything else that man has access to. The effects of these plants on the people who consume them are as varied as the plants themselves. They can be intensely physical, mental, spiritual or a combination of all three, but the experiences usually range from simple physical pleasure and euphoric dreamy states, to conscious journeys spiraling the depths of human awareness. Many indigenous tribes that use such sacred plants believe them to be a gift from God or the Spirit, and their use is a means of communication with God or the Spirit. Some of these plants have unlimited medical potential as well, but their research for the most part is outlawed by the government. The benefits and potential of psychotropic plants are unlimited.

Now on the other hand you have the substances that deserve the real title of drugs. They are synthetic or manmade and chemically altered to produce heightened effects. For the most part they are new and were invented in just the last 100 years or so. These synthetic drugs can be described as any alkaloid that is either chemically altered from its natural form or combined with other chemicals producing an unnatural substance, or any psychotropic plant that has been chemically or physically altered and no longer appears in its natural form and is intended to be consumed by humans, causing temporary changes in perception, consciousness, mood or feeling. These are different from synthetic prescription drugs because the Food and Drug Administration has not approved them for human consumption. There are roughly two different types of illegal synthetic drugs; the first group represents the traditional synthetic drugs such as Heroin, Cocaine,

Crack and Crystal Meth. These are substances that are comprised of dozens of different chemicals, some of which are extracted from plants while others get introduced during the manufacturing process of the drug, either way the total multi-chemical substance is very toxic to the body. All of them are very addictive, meaning the body or mind will crave them after a short period of use, making it very difficult to quit. Even when the user willingly or unwillingly stops taking the drug, they may undergo withdrawal symptoms. The high from these synthetic drugs are almost always of a physical nature, changing the way the body feels either by stimulating or numbing it. Mood change also occurs but is usually in direct reflection to how your body feels. These synthetic drugs have no accepted religious value, and their recreational use is considered to be dangerous and when abused extremely toxic to the human body. The second group is non-traditional synthetic drugs, they represent the substances made from one single chemical or molecule, and that one molecule appears in a high enough quantity so when ingested, it affects mood or feeling in humans. These single molecular synthetic drugs include LSD, DMT and Ecstasy (MDMA). They are relatively harmless to the human body when taken in moderate doses but if consumed in larger quantities they may have adverse mental effects on a user who is unprepared for such an intense experience. Some of these chemicals were originally extracted from plants and then through a chemical process have been altered to a different and now unnatural molecule. These chemical substances are not physically addictive but some users may develop a mental reliance on them because of the happy feelings they create. Of all the different synthetic drugs some were invented by the medical community for medicinal purposes and therefore can have beneficial properties when used properly and administered under the guidance of a medical professional, but others are completely useless and have no beneficial purposes what so ever.

Dividing illegal substances into either synthetic drugs or natural plants is a much more accurate way to classify them. Synthetic drugs can be further sub-classified into less harmful single-chemical substances or more harmful multi-chemical substances. But for all intents and purposes they are both synthetic drugs and bear no resemblance to natural plants. To understand my new drug plan there is really no need to distinguish between types of synthetic drugs, it is only important that you understand the differences between synthetic drugs and natural psychotropic plants. These two categories are important and it is how I will distinguish between illegal drugs throughout the book. Psychotropic plants and synthetic drugs are a perfect and simple way to decipher between good illegal substances that are natural and bad illegal substances that are manmade, ones that should be commercially available and ones that should not be. You should now have a pretty good idea as to what distinguishes a substance from being either a natural growing psychotropic plant or a synthetic chemical psychoactive drug. We are not done yet though, that was just a summery of the two categories. Your understanding of drugs needs to be improved further in order for you to fully grasp this new drug plan. We now need to discuss the drugs individually and thoroughly and see how some of them are directly related to each other and which ones fall under what category. Let's begin with the most frequently used substances and then work our way down to the more obscure ones.

Marijuana is the most commonly used illegal substance, it is a natural psychotropic plant and causes little or no harm to the body. What makes this plant such a burden on society is the fact that it is illegal. This plants historical use dates back to over 4,000 years. The word Marijuana refers to the part of the plant you smoke, which is the flowering tops of the Cannabis Plant. It is these leafy buds that contain the highest concentration of the main psychoactive chemical THC. The herb buds are dried and then shredded for smoking. Today Marijuana is becoming a widely acclaimed therapeutic plant and is gaining acceptance as a medical treatment for many aliments including glaucoma, migraines, pain, stress, loss of appetite, muscle spasms, anorexia and the fatigue and pain suffered by cancer patients who are undergoing radiation therapy. That is just a few but its medicinal possibilities have yet to be completely explored because the government limits the studies allowed since it is an illegal substance. The other uses of Marijuana include recreational and spiritual. It is a psychotropic plant that when consumed allows the user to relax and enter into a peaceful, euphoric state, happy, giddy and rather enlightened by the blissful feelings created by the experience. The effects usually last between one and three hours and then diminish almost completely unless more is consumed. Many modern day users as well as people in past cultures have used the experience created by Marijuana for spiritual purposes. It is the nature of the plant to open up the senses and allow the user to perceive the world from a slightly different perspective then normal, thus maybe bringing them in touch with an inner awareness they lacked before. The plant is used also for inspirational purposes, many people in creative fields such as art, music, writing and philosophy have used the plant to gain a new and unique perspective on their art form. Marijuana is not physically addictive but users can develop a mental reliance on it. Tobacco and Caffeine are far more physically addictive than Marijuana. The ability of Marijuana to alter human perception and judgment even in heavy quantities is less severe than alcohol and for most non-abusers, the more times they ingest Marijuana, the better they get at functioning normally while on it. But it is a psychotropic plant that alters perception, consciousness, mood or feeling, so operating machinery and driving a vehicle should not be under-taken while intoxicated on Marijuana. Marijuana is subject to abuse just like anything else we put in our body, and since Marijuana is a plant that affects the mind, the mind can suffer from excessive use. Just like butter is a food for the body, if you eat a stick of butter every day your body will suffer. Ingesting Marijuana 1-2 times a day is considered heavy use, but it is only those that ingest it 5-7 times a day who exhibit the detached and mind-numbing brain cloud that is seen so commonly in Marijuana abusers. When you smoke Marijuana continuously, you enter into a permanent daze until you take a break, some of this daze however is caused by the toxins in the smoke itself and not by what's in the Marijuana, vaporizing Marijuana limits some of this side effect. A more moderate and acceptable use of Marijuana would be 3-5 times a week. The only negative drawback of this plant is that the most common method of ingestion is smoking it. And when you smoke it, you're ingesting the active chemicals of Marijuana but you're also burning the plant material, which causes it to change so that now you're also inhaling carbon monoxide, tar and other carcinogenic byproducts. You can eat Marijuana but you lose potency unless it is heated up with cheese, butter or other fat-soluble foods. The best way to ingest Marijuana without eating it or smoking it is to vaporize it. Herbal vaporization is a fairly new alternative to smoking, but will eventually be the de facto method of getting a healthy Marijuana buzz. Vaporizing Marijuana is when you put it into a special pipe with a heating element, the Marijuana is heated to a temperature where the oils in the plant are released with the active chemical but the plant matter does not get hot enough to burn. Thus emitting a vapor mist that you inhale just as if you were smoking it, no more harsh smoke on the throat or in the lungs. The Marijuana plant itself can easily be grown indoors or outdoors during the warm seasons. Marijuana is also common in the form of Hashish, which in some ways physically resembles a chocolate bar. It is created in the simplest way by rubbing the flowering tops of the plant with your hands and then collecting the sticky resin and compressing it into a block. It then is smoked as a more potent form of Marijuana. The forming of

Hashish does not change the chemical composition, nor does it add any chemicals to the Marijuana.

Cocaine and Crack are the next most widely used illegal substances. These are just two different substances, which both contain the same chemical that is originally derived from the Coca Plant. The Coca Plant is a natural psychotropic plant that is illegal along with its synthetic representations Cocaine and Crack. Cocaine is actually one of the many active alkaloids in the Coca Plant and when used for drug manufacturing, it is synthetically derived from Coca leaves through a process involving various chemicals and steps. The drug Cocaine is a white powder that has been refined and concentrated into a very physically potent drug, it is most often snorted through the nose or injected via a needle into the bloodstream. Crack is just the freebase form of Cocaine, it is a rock-like substance and is more suitable for smoking, and it too is equally potent. They both contain a very large concentration of the Cocaine alkaloid, making them addictive and in combination with all the other hazardous chemicals in the drugs themselves, extremely damaging to the body. Taking these drugs bring on an intense physical rush that causes some numbness to pain and aggression in the user, it does not affect the mind and consciousness so much as it affects the body. The Coca Plant itself is much more redeeming in nature and has very beneficial properties. It's historical use dates back over 2,000 years. Traditionally, native tribes of South America chewed the leaves to obtain its affects. The leaves not only contain the Cocaine alkaloid but many other nutrients and served as a food that would give them strength and energy during their long hunts through the mountains and jungles. The plant when consumed by humans is harmless and does not exhibit the addictive and destructive properties that synthetic Cocaine and Crack do because it is nowhere near as concentrated, nor does it possess all the unnatural chemical additives that get introduced during the manufacturing process. Coca leaf tea is another means of ingesting the plant, and it is a very popular drink in South American cultures. Its use there is very similar to coffee in America. The Coca Plant is barely anymore psychoactive than the Coffee Plant and to maintain any type of intoxication would require the ingestion of about a dozen cups of tea all drunk within a couple of hours. The Coca Plant has amazing possibilities in the medical realm. In its native region it has commonly been used for aliments such as high blood pressure, altitude and motion sickness, toothaches, fatigue, gastrointestinal upsets, and it also serves as a fast-acting antidepressant. Spiritual use of this plant has always been present in South America where local tribes worshipped it and thanked the gods for giving it to them. The psychotropic Coca Plant has a lot of potential, it is unfortunate that it is illegal, but Cocaine and Crack obviously have very little to no potential at all.

Heroin and Opium are popular drugs and even though they are related there is a big difference between the two. First of all they both come from the psychotropic Opium Poppy Flower, a flower that has been cultivated and used by mankind for over 4,000 years. Heroin is very addictive and damaging to the human body while Opium is much less addicting and not as damaging unless abused frequently over a long period of time. Opium is the raw sap that is secreted when you cut into the seedpod of the poppy flower, it is a milky, white, sticky paste that turns brown or black shortly after being exposed to the air. It is ingested in that natural form and undergoes no processing. Opium contains many alkaloids that have widespread use in the medical community, the two most common of which are Morphine and Codeine, both being synthetically derived from Opium. Heroin is created from pure Morphine through an additional chemical process. The chemicals from the Opium Poppy are haled in the medical community as to be the most effective painkillers available to mankind. Opium can be ingested in a few different ways. Opium tea is fairly common, it is made by crushing dried poppy heads and then brewing them in hot water. Raw Opium sap can be taken orally or rubbed into the skin for pain relief. But smoking the sap is the most common form of ingestion and is typically the method of choice for recreational use. Smoking small quantities can produce euphoric effects that bring peace, tranquility and contentment in the user, relieving stress and ridding the body and mind of physical and emotional pain. Opium can become physically addictive if abused and the body will build up a tolerance after prolonged regular use. Smoking Opium daily for a month will develop into a physical addiction and smoking it three times a day is the sign of an addict. Withdrawing from an addiction to either Opium or Heroin is an unpleasant process. An Opium addict who quits will experience severe flu-like symptoms and depression for 1-2 weeks. It may even take another few months before the addict recovers completely. To prevent a physical addiction to Opium a more moderate and safer smoking practice would be at the most 1-2 times a week. The Opium Poppy has been worshiped by many cultures believing it to be a divine plant from God, given to man to relieve his sufferings. The drug Heroin was first synthesized in the late nineteenth century and is a concentration of Morphine, which is the most addictive alkaloid in the Opium bunch. Heroin is chemically altered to produce almost instantaneous effects once ingested. It is usually a white powder that can be snorted or smoked but most often dissolved in water and injected intravenously into the bloodstream, this method is preferred by most addicts because of the rapid onset. Heroin is a very dangerous substance, it is the most addictive of all the illegal drugs and when abused has devastating effects on the health of the body, but also the mind. Although trying Heroin for the first time will not make someone physically addicted, due to the nature of the experience and the intensity of the rush, the user may seek those same feelings several more times and such repeated use could possibly lead to a physical addiction to Heroin. Ending a Heroin addiction is very painful, especially if the addict is not slowly weaned off the substance. Going cold turkey can be an excruciating and dangerous process. When a Heroin addict quits they become extremely sick, often vomiting and physically weak, at times the body will shake uncontrollably. The extreme physical torture will last for a few weeks but a complete rehabilitation may take several months to a year. Rehab clinics often supplement an addict's

Heroin addiction with Methadone, which is still addictive but satisfies cravings while also having less severe withdrawal symptoms. It is possible to overdose on Opium and Heroin, which in the worst case could lead to death. Just like alcohol there is a definite limit to how much your body can takes at once. The Opium Poppy is a powerful psychotropic plant that should be respected and understood before one ingests its sap. It has very beneficial uses when treated properly but without the proper understanding of the plant one could very easily abuse it and find themselves with an ever growing dependency.

Speed is a category of synthetic drugs, their abuse is also very common. This class of drugs refers to the unnatural and addictive substances known as Speed, pills, uppers, Crystal Meth, Ice, and Glass; it has many other names and types as well. These drugs are more appropriately classified as an Amphetamine or Methamphetamine. They are uppers or drugs that speed up body function and give the user an abnormal increase in energy, sometimes making sleep no longer a requirement for several days at a time. These synthetic drugs have no real base from nature and are usually created from a mixture of several substances including prescription drugs, over-the-counter drugs and weight loss or appetite suppressant drugs. They are very destructive to the body and can be very addictive. However, they are usually more psychologically addictive than physically addictive. Speed is commonly distributed in pill or powder form. The most popular type of Speed is Crystal Meth, which is a whitish pink to light brown powder. It is usually snorted through the nose or smoked but it is also common for people to dissolve it into water and inject it intravenously into the bloodstream. It can become highly addictive after repeated use. Once ingested the user will feel the initial effects almost immediately and they will last between 6-8 hours depending on the amount consumed. The high created could best be described as if you were to drink around 25 cups of coffee all at once, or if you're familiar with Coca Tea then it's like drinking 15 cups all at once. What makes Crystal Meth so dangerous is that the side effects of not being able to sleep or eat can last between 12-24 hours, and when someone ingests it frequently over a period of a few days, their ability to sleep or eat during that time will be greatly affected. The widespread use of Crystal Meth is attributed to the fact that it is a cheaper alternative to Cocaine while still providing a similar experience. All these types of Speed are relatively new drugs and have no religious use by any previous cultures. The only historical use of these drugs was by the military. They would give them to their pilots so that they could accomplish long flights or missions during wartime without needing to sleep. The military also gave them to foot solders to give them more energy and decrease their fear during war engagements. There are some limited uses among the medical community for these types of drugs. They have been prescribed for narcolepsy, appetite suppression and attention-deficit hyperactivity disorder. Their medical use is very limited though and should only be administered by a medical professional. The recreational use of these synthetic substances is dangerous and provides no real benefit to the user.

Ecstasy is becoming more and more popular every year. It is a semi-synthetic drug that's distributed as a pill. Ideally it is pure MDMA, which is a single chemical, but frequently it contains other synthetic drugs such as Speed and Cocaine. These other drugs are added to MDMA to boost the quantity of pills that can be produced from one batch of MDMA as well as making the effects slightly unique to one brand of pill. Sometimes users will never know the difference between a pure Ecstasy pill and one that has been diluted with other drugs. The chemical MDMA was first synthesized around 1912 but the psychoactive effects where not popularized until the 1960s by the famous pharmacologist Dr. Alexander Shulgin. Ecstasy or MDMA is synthetically made from the chemical Safrole, which comes from an oil that is extracted mainly from the root bark of the Sassafras Tree. The oil is about 80% pure Safrole and currently is the best precursor available for manufacturing Ecstasy. Sassafras oil at one time was very common as a food additive or dye and was the original ingredient for flavoring Root Beer, but because it has recently been used for making Ecstasy the government closely monitors its distribution. The oil itself is toxic in large doses but ingesting small amounts has proven to be medicinally beneficial and completely safe. An Ecstasy-like euphoria is not obtainable from consuming plain Safrole, it first must be chemically changed into MDMA before any type of high can be expected. The effects of ingesting Ecstasy can be described best as a physical high that encompasses the entire body with a uniform and intense pleasurable feeling, thus making physical activity and the sense of touch a much more erogenous-like experience. The mind, although not significantly effected, is enveloped with feelings of peace, love and tranquility. Ecstasy is a unique drug in the effect that it loses its ability to stimulate the user after frequent use; it is unlike Heroin and Opium, which after prolonged use a tolerance is developed but can be overcome by simply consuming larger quantities. Instead, with Ecstasy most people can only ingest it so many dozen times before they no longer experience the intense effects. The reason for this is still somewhat unknown and it is not understood if it is a defense mechanism by the body or if the user just becomes too accustomed to the effects to really be overwhelmed and stimulated by them anymore. Most Ecstasy users, probably around 80-90% of them, experience this huge drop off in the effects somewhere between their 5th and 50th session. The effects created by the high and the overall experience is usually cut in half or even lessened further down to 25% of how they originally felt during their first few sessions, and that level of intensity cannot be recovered by taking larger quantities of Ecstasy or by invoking long intervals of time between sessions. Everybody is different and so the drop off in effects hits everyone at different times and whether they lose the intensity after just a few experiences or after their 100th time, it eventually happens. It is a common phrase among Ecstasy users to tell people to enjoy their first few times because they will be the best ones. Once the drop off becomes apparent many Ecstasy users will supplement some of the lost effects with other drugs. They'll take a couple of pills and seeing that they only get roughly half as high, they ingest Speed or Cocaine to bring their Ecstasy experience back up to a more intense level. Ecstasy is not overtly a dangerous drug unless you either combine other synthetic drugs with it, or drink too much water as a reaction to the increase in body temperature that occurs while on the drug, possibly leading to water intoxication. Ecstasy is also not physically addicting but because of the very pleasurable nature of the experience, abusers can develop a mental familiarity with the drug and become reliant on it for feelings of happiness and contentment. In that regard it may cause bouts of depression when a frequent user goes without it for some length of time. There is some spiritual potential in Ecstasy but it historically has never been used for such purposes. Medically it has potential but after making it illegal, the government never granted any research organization permission to experiment with it until just very recently. However, it is theorized that if Ecstasy is administered under the guidance of a medical professional and used sparingly, it could be an extremely effective cure for depression often only requiring a few treatments, coupled with in-depth psychoanalysis it could prove to be a full chemical and mental cure for those plagued with severe depression. Currently MDMA is being tested as an aid in fighting Post-Traumatic Stress Disorder, and as MDMA-assisted psychotherapy for anxiety in advanced cancer patients. Ecstasy or MDMA can be beneficial under certain circumstances, but when very little research is allowed on a substance its effects are not fully comprehended by the scientific community. Subsequently that lack of education translates down to people who buy the drug on the streets and thus because they know so very little about it, they have no basis in refraining from abuse.

LSD, which is also called Acid, is a powerful psychoactive substance; it is considered to be semi-synthetic. The building blocks of LSD are found in nature but for potency value and convenience it is manmade and distributed in an unnatural form. In its pure form it is either white crystalline powder or a clear liquid. LSD is usually distributed on blotter paper, which is an absorbent paper that has been soaked in liquid LSD. One dose is no bigger than one-forth of an inch squared. Sometimes it is also circulated on sugar cubes or candy that has absorbed one drop of liquid LSD, which is also one hit or enough for one person to experience the full effects. Hits are ingested orally. To understand how LSD is made you first must be familiar with where is comes from. LSD is an altered molecule that is extracted from an alkaloid called Ergotamine. The alkaloid comes from a fungus called Ergot that infests rye and other grains. You cannot just ingest the fungus Ergot and expect to have an LSD experience; there are many other chemicals in Ergot that are poisonous. You have to first isolate the main alkaloid and then through an additional chemical process change it to LSD. The manufacturing of LSD requires a lot of chemical knowledge plus access to a fully equipped lab; someone with less than two years of college chemistry could probably not do it. LSD is illegal but what is unique about LSD is that there is a completely natural and almost identical legal form of it called LSA. LSA is a chemical cousin of LSD and produces very similar effects. LSA can be found in psychotropic plants such as Hawaiian Baby Woodrose and some varieties of the Morning Glory Flowers as well as in the Ergot fungus itself. The seeds of Hawaiian Baby Woodrose and Morning Glories can be crushed and then ingested with water to experience their euphoric effects, which are similar to an LSD experience. These seeds have been used in this manner historically by several indigenous tribes for religious ceremonies. Both of these plants are legal and it is very common to see Morning Glory seeds for sale at most garden supply stores. LSD has a lot of medical potential. Before it was banned in the late 1960's due to widespread recreational use, it was believed by some in the medical community to be a treatment for some mental illnesses, depression, criminal rehabilitation and it also served as a very effective cure for alcoholism. The use of LSD was also believed to bring about spiritual experiences. It is a powerful substance that effects mind, body and soul, so without the proper knowledge or atmosphere to experience the drug in, one can abuse it, or more accurately speaking, allow it to abuse them, which subsequently leads to an unpleasant experience. Its effects can be described as hallucinations in the sense that it has the ability to expand sensory perception, leading to an overall state one has never experienced before. LSD is completely non-addictive, the body will not crave the substance and neither will the mind rely on it to function properly. It has no harmful effects on the body when taken in standard doses as well as little or no harm on the mind, unless the user already has preexisting mental disorders. There exhibited immense recreational use in the 1960's that tapered off somewhat but still continues today. Being a drug that greatly affects the mind, LSD is not an easy drug that one could ingest and sit back and let it do all the work like Heroin or Cocaine, LSD will constantly be challenging the users perception and awareness while thrusting them into new levels of thought. Therefore in that respect it has great religious potential. I say LSD is relatively safe but you may not believe that because of the confusion regarding LSD flashbacks. Flashbacks have become a common, negative misperception attributed to LSD. A flashback is when a user believes that they reexperience certain visual characteristics of LSD later in life while not on the drug. But this phenomenon is an extremely rare occurrence and has never been proven to occur in healthy users. People who are epileptic or suffer from a mental disorder are usually the only ones who may exhibit adverse after effects from an LSD experience. If a normal user believes that they experience flashbacks from time to time but they have no mental disorders, then the flashbacks can probably be attributed to optical damage rather than a chemical disturbance in the body. All human eyes see after images, and if someone damages their eyes by consistently staring at bright lights, then they may see after images more frequently then normal because now their eyes are more sensitive to bright colors. To see an after image, you could just stare at a bright red ball for about 30 seconds and then quickly look at a white wall, you will see the after image of the ball except that it will be the opposite color. To understand why this happens you must first know that there are two main light-sensitive cells that are responsible for human vision, they are

Rods and Cones. Rods are mainly used for seeing in low, dark light and they perceive no color information whereas Cones require lots of light but can perceive color. By staring at a particular color the Cone is over worked and the color becomes temporarily "burned" into our eyesight, the after image then slowly fades as we switch to a less intensely colored subject which then allows the Cones to recover. Well, it is the nature of LSD and some other hallucinogens to heighten color perception while on the drug. And what do most people do while on a hallucinogen? They stare at bright lights. Whether they are strobe lights, spinning glow sticks or Christmas lights strung throughout a room, they are all intense bright lights that consistently over stimulate the Cone cells in the users eyes. A lot of times the person on LSD, not knowing better will spend hours staring at spinning bright lights and they do this every time they take the drug. This constant over stimulation may develop into a permanent over-sensitivity within the Cones, making after images appear more frequently and much quicker than normal, thus leading the person to believe that they experience "flashbacks" from time to time. Most of the hallucinogens produce very similar effects in the mind, but you never hear of flashbacks being attributed to mushrooms, Peyote or LSA. It is most likely that the idea of flashbacks was contrived by drug educators to curb LSD use because flashbacks really have no scientific base. LSD for all intents and purposes is a synthetic drug, but the psychotropic plants that contain LSA are natural and legal alternatives to the LSD experience that should not be overlooked by those seeking a similar experience. Psychotropic Mushrooms and the Peyote Cactus create a near identical match to an LSD experience also.

Magic Mushrooms or "Shrooms" are simply the genus of psychotropic mushrooms called Psilocybe. There are other psychotropic mushrooms that produce similar effects such as some species in the genus Panaeolus and Copelandia and the species Amanita Muscaria, but they are less common and usually aren't distributed on the streets for recreational purposes. Psilocybe has somewhere between 100 and 150 species worldwide that when ingested produce euphoric effects in humans. Tribes throughout the world have used these mushrooms religiously for over 2,000 years, referring to them as "Flesh of God." These mushrooms grow naturally throughout the world. There are species of Psilocybe that grow in just about every American state, they're actually very abundant. It is not illegal to have them naturally growing on your property in America, but if you pick them, transport them, ingest them or allow them to dry while in your possession, then you are setting yourself up for possible prosecution. Fresh psychotropic mushrooms are commercially legal in the UK but this is only temporary due to a miswording in the law. However, some other European countries permanently have psychotropic mushrooms legally available. Only expert mushroom hunters track down the psychotropic mushrooms in nature because there are thousands of mushrooms and ingesting the wrong mushroom that you thought was psychotropic, could end up being very poisonous making you extremely ill. You must have a full knowledge of mycology and know how to identify species of mushrooms before you attempt to ingest one that you found in nature. The Psilocybe mushrooms that are common on the drug market are not picked from the wild, they are usually grown indoors by an experienced mushroom cultivator. It is a very easy and inexpensive process to grow these mushrooms indoors at home, you can also grow them outdoors as well, but that is less common because they are more susceptible to being seen by snooping authorities. The effects that Psilocybe mushrooms have on the user are very similar to LSD and Peyote depending on the number of mushrooms eaten. If you consume a light to moderate amount which is about 2-4 mushrooms you will first notice more then likely a body high, a pleasurable warm, tingling throughout your body. You will definitely be happy, maybe slightly giggly and wanting to laugh at everything. Increasing the amount consumed may create mild visual hallucinations, making colors more vivid and surreal. Your mind and thoughts may move at an accelerated speed, jumping from subject to subject with a perspective deeper then normal. Consuming even more mushrooms will become a more intense mental experience, your thoughts will be spiraling around and exploring the depths of your imagination, you may have profound spiritual experiences and great enlightenment or deep confusion from not being prepared and experienced enough for this type of journey. These mushrooms can be very beneficial if respected and used properly in a positive environment. Psychotropic mushrooms have yet to be completely explored by the medical community but they exhibit an ability to be very uplifting, which could possibly bring people out of depression and relieve tension or stress; they may have other medicinal properties as well. The other psychotropic mushrooms besides Psilocybe produce a similar experience but not quite identical to Psilocybe. People who are not emotionally stable should not participate in their consumption. Otherwise there are no mental dangers from ingesting these mushrooms as well as no physical harm either as they are completely non-addictive and non-destructive to the body.

The Peyote Cactus is a natural psychotropic cactus in which its religious use is more common then its recreational use. In America it is an illegal cactus to possess, grow or ingest unless you are an active member of the Native American Church. Native Americans and other indigenous people throughout Southwestern America, and Mexico have used this cactus religiously for possibly 10,000 years. The cactus grows naturally from southern Texas down into Central Mexico. It is a small button cactus with a diameter of about 2-5 inches and rises no more then one inch above the ground. It has a thick carrot-like root that penetrates 8-12 inches into the ground. Peyote is usually consumed by cutting the top button off from the roots and either eating it fresh or dried, usually 4-12 buttons are consumed by one person, they are either eaten plain or made into Peyote tea. There is really no underground drug market for Peyote Cactus because it is rare and not well known among modern drug users, but there has been infrequent circulation of synthetic Mescaline, which is the main active alkaloid in Peyote but it too is rarely available on the drug market. Occasionally LSD pills are wrongfully labeled as Mescaline and circulated among users, most people who do LSD probably couldn't distinguish the difference between LSD and synthetic Mescaline. Peyote is actually legal to grow in other countries such as the UK and Netherlands, but for some reason it is illegal in the US, its natural habitat and place of historical use. The effects of Peyote are somewhat similar to Psilocybe mushrooms and LSD, although the intensity of the experience is in direct correlation to the number of buttons you have consumed. However, it can be a very sacred and spiritual journey that tends to arouse deep inner reflection in the user. The cactus has no physically addicting properties and it does not yield any type of mental reliance. Some of the chemicals inside of the Peyote cactus, especially Mescaline, have intrigued the medical community, but the cactus still suffers from a lack of research so its potential is unknown. The ingestion of the Peyote cactus causes no harm to the body or mind but you should be emotionally stable and well educated about Peyote before trying it.

DMT is a chemical that is naturally found in many psychotropic plants and vines as well as in a North American species of toad. It is usually extracted from its natural source and distributed on the street in a pure and crystal form for smoking. It is pretty rare in today's current underground drug market to be able to obtain pure DMT, as it's not a substance that holds widespread appeal. It did have a surge in popularity during the 1960's but has since all but disappeared. The psychotropic plants that contain DMT have historically and religiously been used for over 2,000 years by indigenous tribes of South America, which is where most of the plants containing DMT grow naturally. These tribes would brew large batches of tea with the plants that contain DMT along with many other psychotropic plants. They would have religious ceremonies involving dance, worship and praise while experiencing the effects of the psychotropic plants. There are really two types of DMT that are found in natural sources, one is regular DMT which has a normal potency and the other is 5-MeO-DMT which is actually around five times more potent. Most psychotropic plants that contain either form of DMT are legal and can easily be purchased through legal entheogens suppliers. But pure DMT that has been extracted from its natural source is illegal. The toad that contains DMT actually secretes it from its poison glands when frightened or agitated; it is pure 5-MeO-DMT that is secreted from the toad. Obtaining pure DMT from the toad requires only a slight squeeze on the poison sacks and they will secrete a white, liquid-like sap, which then can be dried and smoked in that raw form. Smoking the sap destroys any nauseous chemicals that are contained within it, therefore allowing for a full DMT experience to be felt. But simply licking the sap off the toad usually makes the participant pretty sick, frequently consisting of headaches, severe nausea and moderate hallucinations. Extracting the DMT from the toad in this manner yields no harm to the toad, they have plenty of DMT stored up and if you do empty the poison sacks they will quickly refill after a couple of weeks. Traveling through the great American Southwest to find this toad was a popular adventure back in the 1960's for some hippies, who would occasionally even keep the toad as a pet and give it a lavish and plush existence for the remainder of its life. All the toad had to do was give up a little DMT every once in a while. This toad is not endangered and is pretty numerous in its native region. DMT in general is a very powerful substance, whether it is somewhat diluted in tea that you drink or pure DMT that you smoke, it should only be ingested by experienced people. In its pure smoking form its high can be described as a similar but much more intense LSD trip or heavy Psilocybe mushroom experience, but the duration of the effects only last around 20 minutes. It's a quick and compact psychedelic experience while also being one of the most intense ones available to human consciousness. Pure DMT in moderate doses is relatively harmless to the body, it is neither physically nor mentally addictive, though one could experience negative and confusing effects mentally from the experience if not prepared for such a journey. It doesn't have any synthetic additives to it, but depending on the source of the DMT it may have gone through a chemical process in order for it to be extracted. DMT doesn't have any accepted medical value; it is rarely used recreationally because of its intense nature, which leaves only spiritual use as the reason for ingesting it. If a person is experienced with the effects created by these types of substances, then DMT can further expand perception and awareness, which may then help you figure out your existence in the world, leading to what could be a very rewarding spiritual experience. So DMT in its pure form is illegal but the plants and toad that contain DMT are not illegal.

There are a few other drugs that you may or may not heard about, however they only represent a very small portion of users and their distribution is fairly rare. These drugs are called Dissociative Drugs and in some underground markets you may be able to obtain these substances, but in most others and especially the smaller markets, these drugs never make their rounds. I will just give a brief summary since dissociative drugs are nowhere near as widespread as the other drugs and each are similarly dangerous when consumed recreationally. One of these drugs is Special K or Ket, which is the street name, however the medical community knows it as Ketamine, which is an anesthetic. Veterinarians often use it as a cat tranquilizer but it can be used on other small animals as well. When sold on the streets it is most often in the form of a white powder for snorting or smoking. When consumed by humans its effects can be described as hallucinatory, but it is unlike LSD, Mushrooms and Peyote because these promote inner reflection and examination giving one an increased sense of self awareness, whereas Special K is a dissociative hallucinogen, which means the user loses sense of oneself similar to an out of body experience. It is definitely a dangerous substance when abused by humans. A drug very similar to Special K is PCP, also known as Angel Dust. It takes on a liquid form but when sold on the streets it usually has previously been sprayed onto Marijuana, tobacco or other smoking herbs. It too is an anesthetic and a very strong one at that. This is why its users exhibit an extraordinary tolerance for pain while on the drug. The medical community originally used PCP as a surgical anesthetic but because of the negative side effects its medical use has been completely discontinued. PCP like Special K is a very dangerous recreational drug, and they both are controlled substances.

That pretty much sums up the substances that are commonly referred to as illegal drugs. You should have noticed that there are distinguishable characteristics between them and that some are useful and relatively harmless while others are useless and dangerous. And since they all differ so much from each other they really shouldn't all be treated the same. Why is it that a natural growing mushroom is just as illegal as synthetically made Heroin? Or for that matter, why is it that any relatively safe and natural growing plant be grouped together with manmade, addictive chemical drugs? The lack of distinction in modern drug law between substances of little harm and substances of greater harm is probably the single attribute of the Drug War that is most responsible for its ineffectiveness. It is an absurdity to direct resources equally to unequal drugs.

CHAPTER 02: OUR RIGHT TO PLANTS AND OUR BODIES

There is no way to convince me that as a human citizen of this Earth, someone disallowing me from taking a bite out of a natural and native plant is not depriving me of a basic human right. In accordance with Natural Law it would seem that since human beings are natural inhabitants of this earth, they should have the right to grow and consume any plant that is naturally growing on this planet. It then seems unlawful and unethical for a government to forbid a person the private and responsible use of a natural growing Psychotropic Plant, especially when there is surmountable evidence indicating extensive worldwide, religious use of such plants throughout all human existence. It may be the function of the government to oversee and restrict that which is manmade including the unnatural substances that are synthetic drugs, but it is not in the role of the government to rule over and restrict natural plants, which are Mother Nature created. Plants of any kind should not be illegal whether they are poisonous, psychotropic or for nourishment. Man has a natural right to grow and eat the plants of his choice and their possession should not be criminalized and outright banned by any person or government.

For the government to take on the role of deciding which plants we can and cannot ingest, is like them taking on the role of God. It may be the role of someone's God to dictate between what plants they can and cannot eat, but it is not the role of the government. It is the belief of many religions and cultures past and present, that these plants are their sacred right; they have been using them ceremoniously for hundreds and thousands of years throughout the world. The growing and ingesting of these plants is considered to be a symbolic and religious relationship with Mother Nature, the Spirit and God, and these now forbidden plants were once believed to have been given to mankind by God. Since we are no longer allowed access to them, maybe this is why the spiritual nature of man has diminished.

If you are of the Christian persuasion then you may already be familiar with the Bible verse Genesis 1:29 that states: "Then God said I give you every seed-bearing plant on the face of the whole Earth and every tree that has fruit with seed in it. They will be yours for food." God even demonstrated the significance of plants by using them as a test to man and woman by forbidding them from eating the fruit of one tree, and when they failed God punished them. Surely you cannot believe that God gave us these plants just so we can have our elected officials write laws to take them away from us and punish us for growing and using them. The God of the Bible gave man the use of all plants and even though he gave no instructions on their religious use as he did for Wine, there are many religions that hold certain psychotropic plants to be a very valuable religious sacrament. Hindus, Buddhists and Rastafarians all use the Marijuana plant religiously. Some of them incorporate Opium into their spiritual activities as well. Native Americans have long used the Peyote cactus religiously just as many indigenous tribes throughout the world found mushrooms to be of a divine nature. There is hardly a religion on this Earth that doesn't believe in some form or another that we have a right to all plants. The only logical reason for the government to make a law controlling these plants is if they were endangered, but then that law would only forbid the gathering of native plants and not ban their private growing outright like today's psychotropic plant laws do. Most people agree that we as human inhabitants of this Earth, should have the freedom to ingest any foods provided by Mother Nature that we deem fit to eat, so long as that plant or animal has a thriving population and isn't on the verge of extinction.

If the government bans certain plants because it believes that they are harmful to man, why not ban all plants that have a potential to hurt man. There are plenty of poisonous plants out there that are far worse and more destructive to the human body then the psychotropic ones that are illegal. So if the government's general philosophy is that man cannot be trusted to manage for himself the plants of this Earth, then why stop at banning only 5-7 plants. If we are truly that incapable then every plant that has the potential to negatively impact a person should be illegal to grow, possess or consume. I have a black cherry tree in my backyard and its leaves, stems and seeds are very poisonous, but most people do not know that and they might figure that since cherries are fine to eat why wouldn't the rest of the plant be okay. What if one day I decided to make cherry tea with the wilting leaves? I never received a government warning stating that I may have respiratory failure or possibly fall into a coma. I also grow tomatoes and their vines and leaves are also very poisonous. How am I to know that adding a handful of tomato leaves to spice up a salad can make my guests fall ill. The government also never deemed it necessary to let me know that most of my houseplants are poisonous. So if the government feels it is their job to keep me from having certain plants or ingesting them because they are supposedly dangerous, then they are doing a pretty lousy job because I am surrounded by plants that I should not be putting into my body. The fact is they leave it up to us, it is our responsibility to decide what plants we should or should not put into our body. If the government really felt the need to be telling us what plants to eat and not to eat, you would see a label on every fruit, vegetable, plant and seed with their edibility rating. There would be signs posted before you go into national parks about what you should and should not put into your mouth. As you can see it is a huge contradiction to govern over certain plants and not others.

Even if a substance is harmful we still have a right to our body. So in the privacy of our home, if we choose to mix up some strange concoction and consume it, then that should well be within our rights as humans. Regardless if it is a plant or a chemical potion it should be our right to make it and eat it if that is our desire. It could be a nutrient shake that we have created by mixing many fruits and protein blends together or a substance consisting of psychotropic plant extracts and other chemicals. Even if someone just chooses to drink plain dish washing soap, it is still up to the individual to dictate what they put in their body. Prosecuting someone for ingesting a drug is as absurd as charging a person who attempts suicide with attempted murder. However, if the drugged person commits an offense such as public intoxication or driving under the influence while on the drug then they are definitely at risk for prosecution. The government should continue to require the proper health warnings on all commercially sold household items such as cleaning solutions and so forth. And as it is today, those who choose to ingest such a substance should only be subjected to the pain, nausea, expensive medical bills and permanent health damage that accompanies such a decision, and not criminal prosecution. Likewise that should be the law regarding anyone who mixes up their own personal intoxicant and ingests it at home. We have all received decent education on what is toxic to the human body so we know what is harmful to ingest, but with new and revamped drug education, those who seek to get high would have a thorough understanding of how to safely experiment with different intoxicants so as to prevent bodily harm.

Our right to plants and our right to our bodies are both sad casualties of the War on Drugs. Does the government really have to ban some plants for everyone, just to prevent a small minority from turning them into drugs? Do they really need to prosecute people for making and eating something in their own home? It would be more reasonable to allow everyone access to these plants and prosecute only those who abuse them instead of trying to prosecute everyone who uses them. I will define what I mean by abuse later in the book. The government's reasoning for banning these psychoactive substances is because they have a high potential for abuse. But we came to the point a long time ago where crime and violence from prohibition compromises public safety far more than drug abusers themselves. The drug problem is no longer about putting things in our bodies that make us high, it is about the crime and violence that gets fueled by the distribution networks and the prices of drugs, and so we should not be allowed to distribute and make a profit from synthetic, psychoactive substances that have not been approved by the Food and Drug Administration. But if the substance is a natural plant, then it should be freely distributed or possessed so long as the guidelines are followed to maintain public safety, and what a person chooses to do with that plant in their own home is entirely their business.

CHAPTER 03: AMERICA'S GIFT TO THE WORLD: A FAILED DRUG WAR

America's got a drug problem. No big deal so does the rest of the world. Every country has its fair share of drug users this is really nothing new. For all of human existence people have been getting high on some kind of substance or another, whether it's psychotropic plants or more recently synthetic drugs there is no denying that it has indeed always been a trait of mankind, and whether you view it as a hindrance or a developmental procedure, it will nonetheless never go away. It is not shameful to have a certain percentage of your population that ingests drugs, in fact it is completely natural. People have all sorts of reasons for doing so, some more admirable than others. What isn't natural though is how we have decided to deal with drug use. We have only more recently been taught that it is shameful and a destructive practice that needs to be diminished at all costs.

Drug use today is only a burden on society because of the method we have set about in dealing with it. By choosing this path of banishment and outlawing drugs and psychotropic plants, we have created the underground drug market of today. It is corrupt and violent but serves the purpose of getting drugs to those who want them and fulfilling that demand. This does not mean that we should just consent to all evils of society just because a small group of people want it and are going to do it regardless. Drug use is different, it isn't preying on others or harming them, it is a self-inflicted act. What makes it harmful to others is the ubiquitous crime that is caused by our current drug law, which propelled the drug trade underground. Combine that with the lack of truthful education on drugs and psychotropic plants, users have no grounds to make educated decisions on the drugs they choose to use. It is no surprise that we are stuck in an on going fight that continues to be a waste of money and resources and bears no end in sight.

America has attempted to abolish drug use the same way it tried to abolish alcohol during the early twentieth century, with zero tolerance for its existence whatsoever. But what we should have learned from alcohol prohibition is that banning popular intoxicants only leads to widespread crime and violence, and it is only when you lift the ban and regulate the substance that the crime and violence disappears. Although there is violence and often death that is still attributed to alcohol, mainly from drunk driving, it will exist whether alcohol is legal or illegal. What diminishes when legalized is the enormous amount of crime and violence that plagues a nation through illegal distribution and the financial cost of combating the substance. The criminal activity that follows drug prohibition is far more devastating on society than the abuse of the substance itself. Legalizing and regulating psychotropic plants will still bring some abuse of them, but the abuse already exists and even when legal, the effects of substance abuse on society will never compare to that which is caused by the underground drug market. It is the crime and violence of distributing the substances that will diminish once legalized, but as always, substance abuse has to be combated with education and if that fails then through effective punishments. Wasting money and resources by persecuting people who simply use drugs should not be a part of any drug plan. Today we persecute drug users far beyond what is reasonable when really all they are doing is putting something in their body, which in all reality is a right not a crime. But there is no reality in our drug law, we don't allow the existence of drugs, we don't allow people to take drugs and we don't allow people to distribute drugs, but meanwhile all that still goes on and what we are left with is a nonsensical Drug War.

Unfortunately America has become the propagator of bad drug laws. At one point the world dealt with drug and psychotropic plant use with a bit of complacency. Getting high had no grave effects on society and limited impact on the individual. There was some money to be made in drug distribution but it was very minor, nothing like the unlimited potential for financial gain of today. It is now because of the government's choice to deal with it in this ineffective manner, one of the largest industries on the planet, all that money continuously supporting crime and corruption. But instead of the US government keeping its own drug ideals and problems to itself, it has expanded its Drug War beyond its borders and with the aid of a few other western countries, has spread this ineffective drug policy throughout the world. Like an over powering bully it has used its influence and bargaining position to demand others follow suite. America has used its dominance to make sure its neighbors and allies fall into compliance. Canada perhaps would have legalized Marijuana quite a while ago had it not been for the American governments' threats. Canada knows keeping Marijuana illegal leads to more crime, wasted money, and unnecessary prosecutions, they know that Marijuana is less addictive than tobacco and less debilitating and harmful than alcohol. They know that the majority of Canadians also support legalizing Marijuana. But even when they try to decriminalize it further or make it legal to possess even small amounts, the American government makes its usual threats that could drastically affect free trade and travel between the two countries. So now most Canadian provinces have Marijuana listed as a minor controlled substance and the law is usually only enforced when large amounts of Marijuana are being grown or distributed. There are a lot of pressures that the American government can apply to its neighbors and allies to keep them from easing up on the Drug War.

Even International bodies have been persuaded to help fight the Drug War. They have adopted the idea that all drug distribution must be stopped and to do so you must rigorously go after the drugs and their users, but also destroying and banning the plants that drugs come from is just as important. The UN has passed international laws banning the distribution and spread of the Coca Plant and almost all other psychotropic plants that synthetic drugs come from. As they see it, the practice of outlawing plants is just another tool in stopping the spread of drugs and cutting into drug dealer profits, but it actually does the opposite. It confines the plants to one sector of society and that sector is a corrupt minority looking to gain power. How they gain power is by making and selling drugs for a large profit, this money goes on to fuel their underground activities and finance their causes. Banning plants allow criminals to use them for profit but it is also an unfortunate step down the path of taking away personal freedoms. If this practice is not reversed then banning additional human rights is that much easier.

The obsession by those in high governmental positions to eradicate all drug use has clearly gotten out of hand, when there are countries like China and Singapore that execute several dozen people each year for non-violent drug offenses and other countries including America that lock people up for more then five years for habitually using drugs. With the skyrocketing price of the Drug War itself, it only makes sense that we reevaluate the entire situation. Everyone involved in the fight against drugs is plagued with tunnel vision. They can no longer look at the Drug War and determine an adequate solution for the problems it causes. The only solution they perceive is to get tougher and tougher on drug users and drug distributors. But it does not matter how hard your stance on drugs is, because even if you enact tougher drug laws that punish drug users even more, or lock up drug distributors for 20 years and more aggressively go after the drug cartels, it will not stop the profits or the crime that is attributed to drugs. Dwindling the supply of drugs will increase the prices of drugs, so the dealers will still always get their profits and because those profits are guaranteed to be high, dealers will violently protect their lucrative business. Plus drug abusers and junkies will always be forced to rob and steal in order to afford drugs. The only way for the Drug War to find success through eradication is by being 100% effective, and to do that would require the removal of all drugs and their plants from the Earth. Removing anything less than 100% of all drugs and psychotropic plants would make that small amount left extremely profitable for those who manufacture and distribute them. When drugs are illegal and profitable, crime is always the by-product. That is why the Drug War will never come close to being successful. Even with the hundreds of billions of dollars spent every year, more than two-thirds of drugs still get through to the streets. There is not enough money or resources for any government to be able to stop all drugs from being made locally or smuggled into their country. They would have to spend over ten times the current amount to even be moderately successful and the only way for a government to come up with that much excess money would be to sell drugs themselves.

If the War on Drugs has taught us one thing it's that now is the time to reexamine the polices that propel it, because after over 100 years of drug prohibition there are absolutely no changes in drug culture or the underground drug market; they both are thriving. Drug culture is rampant and has carved out a niche within every community worldwide. Unfortunately, that niche causes some havoc on the surrounding community because the users have never been properly educated about drugs and psychotropic plants. So users have a tendency to abuse these substances, and with the local crime that always follows the demand for drugs, you end up with a problem that affects all of society everywhere, a problem that the Drug War has had little effect in curing.

CHAPTER 04: WHY GET HIGH?

Why a person chooses to use drugs or a psychotropic plant is really a question only they can answer, however the reasons are endless. There are the noblest of reasons such as religious and spiritual practice followed by medicinal use then recreational use, but then there are also the negative reasons like addiction and escapism. Only the individual user can answer that question of why. Why do they choose an alternate temporary reality as opposed to the normal reality of existence that most people experience all their lives? If you were to ask your typical federal drug employee why people take drugs, they'll usually respond in a predictable manner by repeating what they've been taught or what reasons they perceive. Something along the lines of, "People do drugs because they can't deal with their problems, they take drugs to escape from reality and numb the pain of their troubled life." He would then go on to say, "You see when people are high nothing else matters, they don't have to worry about paying the bills anymore, they can forget about their job and it doesn't matter, no more responsibilities, because their head is just floating up there in the clouds, everything feels good, everything is fine when you're on drugs." That federal drug employee will then probably end with a closing statement somewhat resembling the following, "They get so high everyday that they no longer care that their drug use is causing havoc on their health and everyone around them and not to mention society, all they care about is getting that next fix, and they now have an addiction in which they will sacrifice everything to feed." That is a pretty negative outlook on drug use and although you certainly cannot apply it to all drug users, it does have some truth. To stereotype all drug users under those reasons is irresponsible. Realistically less then 10% of drug users abuse drugs in that way. That leaves over 90% of drug users who take drugs for other reasons. In this chapter we will examine the many possible reasons why people ingest drugs and psychotropic plants.

All drugs and psychotropic plants have different qualities to them, that is they all create different experiences for the user. Some of these substances create similar highs while others create highs that are unique to that substance only. But it is the large range of effects between all the drugs that gives the user many intoxicating choices. Some users will experience these effects differently than other users. Even if they both have taken the same substance and the same amount of that substance, each user may have very different outcomes or highs. It probably has a lot to do with our body make up, our education about the substance, and our expectations regarding the outcome. No one person is wired the same as another, and no one has the same brain chemistry or physical attributes. So different substances and chemicals may be absorbed and processed in a manner somewhat unique to the individual. Same with education and expectation, if you don't know what to expect or prepare for, then your experience may be different from if you did have a general knowledge about the substance before you ingest it. However, none of these substances produce profoundly different experiences from person to person. They do have an overall uniform effect on all humans but the separate experiences may be perceived differently due to preconditions. Everyone who ingests these substances does so because they are attracted to an individual characteristic of the substance. It is that characteristic of the substance which affects the user by temporarily changing perception, consciousness, mood or feeling. These temporary changes are what comprises the high that the user experiences. Out of all the different highs available, the drug one chooses is a good indicator of their motive for getting high. Unfortunately government education has taught us that there are only a few motives for getting high. We know that story line, it's all about escaping pain and getting spaced out. But the real reasons for ingesting drugs and psychotropic plants are as diverse as the number of people who ingest them. Technically every single person has a different reason for ingesting the substances that they do and so logically there could be over 200 million reasons and motives, because that's about how many people ingest illegal drugs today on the planet. A lot of people share some of the same reasons though and the majority of people use drugs in a positive manner. All your life you were taught the extreme worst cases of drug use, the most damaging health effects, the irresponsible user, and the government took all these preposterous warnings and applied them to all drugs. You never really learned about any of the historical or religious application of illegal psychotropic plants, and definitely nothing about beneficial medical purposes or recreational uses similar to alcohol. Therefore most people look down on all drug use, and although some usage is irresponsible and dangerous, the majority is harmless and has only been provoked into becoming harmful by the laws set about to discourage it. One cannot benefit from the substances they ingest when they are always cast into paranoia, surreptitious scrutiny and the underground dealings that have become the only method for obtaining these substances. Drugs and psychotropic plants have been exiled from society and all its participants deemed degenerate criminals. It is amazing that any drug users rise above the negative disarray and use these substances in a positive manner. Thankfully most of them do, because if all drug users were hopeless junkies and all illegal substances were as harmful and addictive as they say, then we would have no choice but to continue a Drug War that hunts down all drugs, all drug users and all drug distributors and imprisons the offenders indefinitely.

Some people seek a high apart from alcohol because alcohol does not make you high, it makes you drunk, it's a depressant, a stupefier and these people solicit feelings other than those created by alcohol. 'To be' or 'to get high' means almost anything but it has become the generally accepted term that describes the effects created by certain substances that alter mood and feeling. 'High' in reference to drugs has acquired a negative connotation. To most people who haven't ingested any drug or psychotropic plant it plainly means doped, drugged, euphoric, drunk or inebriated, to have your head in the clouds and nothing matters except that current moment in which your reality and senses are altered, to them it means a sacrifice of health over pleasure. You can get high from almost anything, and everything creates different effects. You can get high on synthetic drugs, psychotropic plants or by inhaling the toxic fumes of spray paint and other noxious chemicals. You can also get high on religion, meditation, sex, and exercise or by simply depriving your brain of oxygen. The methods of getting high are universally known, but the reasons for doing so are more of an enigma because most people do not understand what feelings are actually created when you get high, so they do not understand why people choose to ingest these substances.

We know the main reasons why people ingest psychotropic plants or synthetic drugs, they are primarily for spiritual, recreational or medicinal purposes. But that tells us very little regarding motive and what the user may indeed derive from the use of such substances. Then of course there are the more negative reasons too. I will dissect all these reasons and examine them in more detail.

When you ingest a substance that makes you high, whether it is a psychotropic plant or a synthetic drug, it alters your state of awareness. Normal awareness or your everyday waking reality is what you are accustomed to; it is the awareness that most people live in their entire life, other than the times when they ingest moderate to large quantities of alcohol. Everyone is very accustomed to his or her own normal awareness, it dictates how they think or how fast they comprehend and respond, and to what degree they imagine and invent. It is usually the same all the time unless inflicted by burdensome emotions or hormones. This normal awareness has bred complete confidence in one's own senses, the individual fully understand the input gathered by the senses and they accept their limitations as well. That is because we are all conditioned to accept our senses for what they are and with good reason because they are very advanced and there is no justification to believe that they can sense more than they actually do. The view towards our minds is also the same. Why should we believe that our mind could think differently or faster and more efficiently, or connect with things on deeper levels making us more capable in decoding the hidden truths of our world? We are more than willing to accept that our senses and mind can be degraded and as time goes by it is all the more apparent, we simply know it to be a fact of life. But why is it so hard to imagine that our senses and mind can expand their ability to perceive if only for just a few short hours at a time. There are of course substances that dull the senses and the mind too, the most common of which is alcohol. It is the dulling or the expanding of the senses and the mind that leads to an altered awareness or reality in the individual and this is the experience created by the drug or plant.

Drugs are not the only things that alter our awareness; injury acts on the senses and alters them the same way love, anger and other emotions act on the mind and alter it. Depending on their degree of infliction our awareness or reality is slightly obscured. Although drugs have a much quicker and more intense ability to alter awareness, as you can see the process is not unique to them only. These illegal substances present a vast assortment of different feelings for the user to experience. There is a drug or plant that will affect every sense and every characteristic of the mind. With these substances you have the ability to expand that sense or that facet of your mind, or you can dull the sense and your mind. What determines which feelings a user will indulge in and regularly experience, is usually in direct reflection to the circumstances of their life and how much education they've received regarding that particular substance.

Now to understand these highs in a more accurate sense we will have to look at the reasons why these substances are ingested and examine all the scenarios for which an individual chooses to partake in their use. How and why does someone use illegal substances for religious or medicinal purposes? How and why do they use them recreationally and what differentiates positive recreational use from negative recreational use? What is felt in the mind and body of the user when they create their alternate reality and how does it act on perception, consciousness, mood or feeling to create these highs? I will answer all these questions in the following, starting with the positive uses and then moving into the negative uses.

Religious drug use sounds like an oxymoron but that is because drugs aren't used religiously, plants are. Religious psychotropic plant use is a much more accurate statement when describing the spiritual pursuits that some people undertake while on reality altering substances. You would be hard pressed to find anybody who actively takes the harsh, synthetic drugs for religious or spiritual purposes; this is because it is the nature of most synthetic drugs not to bring about easily obtainable forms of enlightenment. Some people may occasionally have a spiritual experience while on or coming down from an addictive synthetic drug. But it is usually in direct response to an overwhelming experience that occurs from a near overdose or short-term heavy abuse of the drug. When the user finally emerges, it is the disgust and fear from their over indulgence and dangerous ways that may lead to a life-changing or eye-opening experience. Most of the synthetic drugs have near zero ability to bring about spiritual experiences by themselves. On the other hand every single psychotropic plant has an enormous amount of historical evidence regarding their religious use. So when you hear of drugs being used for spiritual purposes, it is almost exclusively in reference to psychotropic plants, however since these plants are outlawed in the same way that synthetic drugs are, they all get grouped together under that one category. So while describing the practices of spiritual use I will only be referencing psychotropic plants since most synthetic drugs are not applicable to this method.

It is indeed true that a wise man never looks at the world the same way twice, and although there are many ways to alter your perception of the world, psychotropic plants provide an immediate and obtainable bend in your normal reality. So you can then experience that alternate awareness and view your life, the world and possibly all existence a little differently, maybe leading to an enlightenment which could thus possibly expand your once rigid and fixed awareness. It is this altering of perception, consciousness and feeling that brings about spiritual experiences in the user. These experiences may lead them closer to God, and it may give them a profound understanding of all existence or help them learn more about their own mind and body. Whatever the outcome, the user feels a satisfaction that speaks to the soul. Not all common psychotropic plants alter consciousness so deeply though; there is a pleasant variety of plant-induced experiences ranging from euphoric to intense.

A mild euphoria is obtainable from Marijuana while others such as Opium create physical pleasure and mental tranquility, but then there are the plants that take you on full-blown journeys through your consciousness. The stronger psychotropic plants that produce these types of experiences are primarily psychotropic mushrooms, the Peyote Cactus and plants that contain DMT or LSA. These are the natural substances that are most responsible for religious experiences. In today's modern drug classification they are called hallucinogens, but the term hallucinogen is very misleading. Its definition plainly put, means to perceive things that are not there or to have stimuli that doesn't come from an external source but rather from an internal mental disorder or from drug ingestion. If you have never ingested these types of substances then thinking of them as hallucinogens is probably the only way for you to understand them, but if you do have experience with them then you'd know that a more accurate description would be to say that they have an ability to expand sensory perception. That is, flooding your senses with much more information than is normally available while also forcing your mind to consciously think in a new way, it indeed is a very challenging experience. It is during the experience that the user attempts to make cohesion out of the surge of random input and it is how they assemble their understanding of this new experience that will determine what exactly they will learn from it. This is why these substances are called the mind-expanding drugs. If someone possesses the ability to adequately process all this new information that they experience while on the substance, then they will more than likely gain a certain degree of knowledge from the experience. Because the senses are wide open and sensing all this new input, it is very likely that the user will experience a direct connection with God, the universe or themselves that they have never had before. All that these "hallucinogens" are doing is busting down the barriers of our normal senses and allowing us to perceive the world a little differently. What we make out of this new world will dictate its effect on us. It takes a pretty brave person to explore the inner self in such a manner, which will not appeal to many, but if everyone is educated on the effects of these plants then it is likely few will abuse them and most will choose not to participate in psychotropic plants that produce such intense experiences. Even with the intense experiences that some of these psychotropic plants can cause, they still should not be withheld from the private individual. These substances in the broadest sense allow you to communicate in new ways with your mind, body, and soul, while providing you with an extended understanding of those human aspects. That is of course if you are experienced enough and able to use them in this proper manner. You can still ingest these same substances for non-spiritual reasons and that is what a large percentage of hallucinogens users do. If you choose not to use these strong psychotropic plants for internal exploration, then they can become recreational endeavors by ingesting smaller quantities. Ingesting smaller amounts of these plants will provide a euphoric high that is more intense than Marijuana but possesses no deep or profound qualities, just a nice and casual, upbeat intoxication.

Spiritual and religious use of psychotropic plants is a commendable reason to ingest these substances. People who are willing to dive into their own consciousness and experience the world in perceivably altered ways are really just modern explorers. Their tools for exploring inner space are psychoactive substances, whereas man uses other tools to explore the external world such as ships, spacecrafts and microscopes. There is no difference other than the fact that you can't launch a space shuttle into human consciousness, so instead you rely on substances that bring human consciousness to a much more vivid and explicit state. During your trip into your own awareness it may indeed be God or the Spirit that you come into contact with and are able to communicate more directly with. But denying man access to some of these natural tools is no different from denying him access to microscopes and spacecrafts or even books and bibles for that matter.

Using drugs and psychotropic plants for medicinal reasons is a very valid choice for ingesting them. Unfortunately drugs are used medicinally a whole lot more than psychotropic plants. Obviously I'm including prescription drugs with that statement, but nonetheless you just don't see doctors recommending natural psychotropic plants for any type of human suffering; it is always a synthetic drug that they prescribe. Not many people choose to use illegal synthetic drugs for medicinal purposes, but there is a growing number of people who self-administer psychotropic plants to help ease their health problems. Illegal synthetic drugs are not prescribed medically at all anymore, there was a time when some were used in such a manner and for a while they were considered very effective. It is in fact the medical community who is responsible for developing many of today's synthetic illegal drugs, but modern research has shown that they are far more hazardous than helpful. It is rather sad how neglected psychotropic plants have become in our modern society, especially in regards to medical applications. In turn we have become all too reliant on synthetic prescription drugs. People use psychotropic plants to ease many different illnesses or sufferings, but I am only going to list a few examples because listing them all would double the size of this book. Besides in the minds of most people it would be little more than speculation, since there is very little scientific evidence that backs up the use of psychotropic plants for such medicinal purposes. This could quite possibly be because the substances are illegal and the government never took the time to study them for such use, before banning them all outright and disallowing their study by anyone. However, there is an enormous amount of historical evidence as well as unlimited personal accounts by people who found these plants to be extremely beneficial in easing their suffering.

With psychotropic plants there exists the possibility that an individual can self-administer all their own medicine, no longer needing to rely on synthetic over-the-counter or prescription drugs. Some people are already aware of this but for others all it will take is a little education, so that they too will know how to use these plants to ease and maybe cure their sufferings. Psychotropic plants provide natural medicine and are free if you grow them yourself. This prospect definitely scares the legal drug industry and keeps them lobbying against any type of legalization. Usually only a small quantity of a psychotropic plant is ingested in order to ease a medical condition. This small amount proves to be medicinally beneficial without causing the person to get overtly high. Sometimes however, it is desirable to feel uplifted and high while the suffering is being eased and for that reason psychotropic plants are an attractive medicine to a lot of people. Here are some of the more common medicinal uses of psychotropic plants: for pain relief, Marijuana or Opium is often ingested. For headaches and appetite stimulation Marijuana is also useful. For depression a person may use Marijuana or Mushrooms and for nausea or fatigue, Coca tea is useful. Really if a person is knowledgeable enough they could use psychotropic plants to ease most ailments that they encounter throughout the course of their lifetime.

The Recreational use of illegal drugs is a very broad reason for choosing to ingest them, but it is also the most widespread intention for their consumption.

There are many degrees of recreational use ranging from responsible to dangerous. So it may help to understand why people would use illegal substances recreationally by comparing them to the recreational use of alcohol. The ingestion of alcohol also has varying degrees of use ranging from responsible to dangerous. It is not necessarily alcohol or the drug itself that is prone to abuse, it is the individual who is prone to abusing them. People don't just wake up one morning and decide to abuse intoxicating substances. It all stems from the circumstances of their life. Depending on their social status, their ability to rise above their surrounding negative influences and how educated they are about the substances, are all factors that dictate whether the person will be prone to abusing these substances or use them in a responsible manner. Now of course there are a couple of substances that are more prone to abuse than others, Heroin and Opium. Unlike the other substances where the user willfully chooses to abuse them, these two without the proper education can incite abuse more easily. That is why education is extremely important in order to encourage people to stay away from making their own synthetic Heroin, and if they do use Opium to use it responsibly.

So let's first examine why illegal substances are used recreationally in a responsible manner. Now I am not going to suggest that it is possible to use addictive, synthetic drugs in a positive, recreational way; this would be without question a fabrication on my part. Most of them are just too toxic to the human body to have any redeeming characteristics whatsoever, and their highs do not create uplifting and enlightening experiences. But still many people insist on indulging in them. The simplest explanation is that they seek to get high and since they have no real drug education or safe alternatives that are readily available, they just go with whatever they can get no matter how dangerous they are. I will explain synthetic drug use in more detail later in this chapter when I tackle the issue of dangerous recreational use because that is really what most synthetic drug use falls under. That leaves us with the responsible and recreational use of psychotropic plants. Because psychotropic plants are natural and do not undergo any type of chemical process, they are a much safer alternative to synthetic drugs. And so they can be easily and enjoyably used in a recreational manner, while also maintaining a high probability for responsible use. Clearly psychotropic plants aren't immune from abuse, but the physical harm that arises from such abuse is somewhat limited since they are natural substances.

Getting high for the fun of it is what defines recreational use and when it is undertaken responsibly, the reasons for doing so are no different then the reasons for responsibly consuming alcohol. These reasons include celebratory, relaxation, and social enjoyments as the main purposes for their consumption in this regard. Many people also get high on various substances to enhance their chosen form of entertainment. For visual entertainment like movies or light displays some will ingest psychotropic mushrooms or other so called hallucinogens because they can make colors more intense or vivid, similar to turning up the saturation in our eyesight. For audio entertainment a little

Marijuana is often ingested to bring the music to a more explicit state; depending on the user it may allow them to connect with every beat and feel the rhythm more profoundly. For some, ingesting Marijuana prior to sex is occasionally desired because it broadens the senses allowing for a more pleasurable experience or a deeper connection with their partner. There is really no set way to experience these types of substances, it is really up to the user to experiment and find what highs they enjoy best and what activities if any that they like to partake in while high. As long as they don't ingest really enormous amounts of the substance all at once, ingest it so frequently it becomes a distraction from their everyday responsibilities or use it to fuel negative and destructive behavior, then they are using these substances in a proper, recreational manner.

The exact opposite of responsible use of illegal substances is dangerous use of them, or using them for negative purposes or over indulging in them and allowing them to be abused, thus causing harm to the body and neglecting one's responsibilities. Most commonly it is synthetic drugs that are used in this manner but psychotropic plants can be abused like this also. Smoking Marijuana 5-7 times a day everyday is an example of over use or abuse and so is smoking Opium so frequently that you develop an addiction. But the synthetic drugs that are most devastating when abused are Heroin, Cocaine, Crack, and Crystal Meth. What leads someone to abuse these drugs? Again it is the circumstances of the users life that dictates their desire to abuse them. Although not always true in every case, it is usually someone with nothing to lose or gain in life who is most likely to find comfort in the abuse of drugs. Let's examine this type of abuser further. Most people know what a junkie is and they know there are significant differences between a junkie and a pothead. A junkie for the most part is someone who abuses Heroin, they have developed an overwhelming addiction to the drug and their only motivation in life is to get more Heroin in order to satisfy their cravings. People usually turn to Heroin because of circumstances, that is they have lost their job, their house and possessions, they're usually living on the streets and are subjected to all the crime and torment that accompanies that life. Sometimes these people were abused as children, needless to say they are at the end of their rope and so they turn to Heroin because they have nothing else to lose. Heroin then allows them to escape their misery and feel good while doing it. It is a drug that has devastating effects on the body but they do not care because they've concluded that there is nothing else to live for and the faster death arrives, the better. These are the people that society has left behind, there are not enough government resources to adequately help these people and the programs that do exist manage to only be effective a small percentage of the time. Junkies can also be people who abuse Cocaine or Crystal Meth regularly, it is really anyone who abuses the worst types of illegal substances and has no current desire to discontinue use. People who abuse Crack are more commonly called crackheads but they too are junkies because they have decided that the effects of their synthetic drug is worth the health risks. Sometimes they believe these because prior to becoming addicted, they received very little proper drug education and never knew the harmful effects. However, the main reason they don't care about the health risk is because they are stuck in a negative existence in which they believe they cannot escape and so they hopelessly turn to drugs. For example, let's look at the ghetto, typically a very low-income community with a high minority population. The streets run rampant with gangs and criminal activity while the majority of the housing complexes are run down. This is a perfect place to proliferate dangerous and profitable drugs. The vast majority of youth in the city feel trapped and their family cannot afford to send them to college. Usually after being raised in such a dangerous urban environment they have long lost their desire to excel in life. In its place has developed complacency, they now accept the fact that this is their life and they will never escape it. So they indulge in the life style of crime and selling drugs and to cope with the negativity of it all they seek out drugs such as Crack that numb the senses. There is only one way for the government to aid these types of communities and that is flood them with money, but the government has no extra money to do so. If there were no ghettos then there would probably be 90% less crackheads in this country. The government needs to go into these excessively poor communities and raise the standard of living, build better schools, add some new beautiful parks and create better housing facilities. No one or very few can possibly have any motivation to succeed in life when they are raised in a violent and deplorable community that resembles a prison more than it does a healthy city dwelling. This is what causes a lot of people to abuse drugs, they have no choice; they are trapped in their run-down community and receive unacceptable education from an under-funded and deteriorating school. They have very little resources to help them rise above and so they succumb to the life and endure the negativity and pain on a daily basis, and nothing numbs pain and allows you to forget your troubles better than dangerous addictive drugs.

There are all sorts of reasons for ingesting drugs, and since we do have a right to our bodies, if someone sees their life as being so miserable that the addictive and repetitive use of alcohol, sedatives or painkillers are what they deem necessary to help them cope with their tormented existence, then they have the right to do so. But it is the role of the government to help prevent people from degrading down to this level and to educate them so that they have a knowledge base to make wise decisions regarding the substances they put in their body. The government will have the resources to accomplish this once the Drug War is ended. If someone chooses to privately ingest a psychoactive substance for medicinal, spiritual or recreational reasons then they should not be prosecuted for doing so.

CHAPTER 05: FUTURE U.S. DRUG POLICY

The objective of this new policy is to end the Drug War, not by caving in to the drug culture and making everything legal but through enacting sound policies that reconcile every aspect of the controlled substance problem. The Drug War in its current state is not practical and can never be won. To win the Drug War we must either abolish the desire that people have to ingest drugs or eliminate the drug distributors by substantially decreasing their profits. Since it is improbable to change the human demand for drugs, we instead pursue the supply. The current method is to intercept large shipments of drugs before they get to their destination. But this is ineffective because most drugs get through anyway. Even if the supply is somewhat cut, then the prices of drugs go up, so the drug distributors obtain their high profits no matter how many shipments are intercepted. It is also illogical to go after the plant source of drugs by attacking the crops in their native countries; the world is just too big to track down and destroy all psychotropic plant fields and locate all indoor crops. There isn't enough resources as it is, plus more than likely it will target poor, local farmers who aren't connected with drug manufacturing and distributing.

The only way to end the Drug War is by making drugs unprofitable for those who illegally distribute them, and curb abuse by promoting honest education about the substances themselves. To accomplish that the government must allow people to privately eat psychoactive substances and as long as we educate them openly and vigorously they will be able to do so responsibly. So with that in mind let's look at the basics of how this policy can be formed.

Basing our belief that all human beings have the right to grow and consume any plant that is naturally growing on this planet, and with that they also have a right to their body, we must enact written law to protect these rights while also maintaining public safety standards. If that is done correctly then the War on Drugs will end. Wording the law is not a tough challenge once the general concepts are understood. There are really only two practices in my drug philosophy for the government to uphold, they are to allow the existence of psychotropic plants and to punish those who distribute synthetic drugs for profit. As long as those two practices are upheld, the smaller details of the law are really only trivial. The goal of this drug plan is to save the majority of the money already being spent on the Drug War, allow for a new and substantial income for the government created through taxation of psychotropic plants, and to dissolve the underground drug market by making it unprofitable. To do all that you must allow people to grow a number of psychotropic plants that is appropriate for personal use. The actual quantity is not greatly important, however there needs to be a limit so as to separate private and commercial growers. Keeping a quantity limit on psychotropic plants for personal use also helps prevent the easy mass production of synthetic drugs from these plants. Commercial growers or large-scale cultivators have to possess the proper licensing for the amount of psychotropic plants that they will be producing. All commercial distributors will have the proper licenses to sell psychotropic plants and their natural products as well.

You should now have a good understanding of what illegal drugs are, as well as be able to decipher between psychotropic plants and synthetic drugs. We have established that humans have a fundamental right to grow and ingest any plant of our choosing, and couple that with the right to our bodies, we can ingest a harmful substances too if that is our wish. But what we don't have a right to do is distribute synthetic drugs that have not been approved by the Food and Drug Administration and make a profit off them. With the legalization of all psychotropic plants there needs to be some restrictions and regulations to maintain public safety; the law will follow these basic principles:

1. Allow for the private and responsible use of psychotropic plants.
2. Require state licensing for the commercial growing and distribution of psychotropic plants.
3. Prevent distribution of psychotropic plants to minors.
4. Prevent public intoxication and maintain driving restrictions.
5. Maintain the illegal status only on distributing synthetic psychoactive drugs for profit.

Let's look at how the law should be written and its possible implications. Each basic principle will be examined in detail with the corresponding law. At the conclusion of each law will be a summery and how it applies to everyday use. The following definitions will be held true throughout each law.

Definitions:

Psychotropic Plant: Any naturally growing fungus or plant or parts of plants including fruits, leaves, seeds or secretions that when consumed by humans, causes temporary changes in perception, consciousness, mood or feeling.

Natural Psychotropic Plant Product: Any unaltered and desirable part of a psychotropic plant that is in its final, natural form and ready for consumption.

Synthetic Drug: An alkaloid that is either chemically altered from its natural form or combined with other chemicals producing an unnatural psychoactive substance. Or any psychotropic plant that has been chemically or physically altered and no longer appears in its natural form and is intended to be consumed by humans, causing temporary changes in perception, consciousness, mood or feeling.

Minor: Persons under the age of 18.

Principle 1: Allow for the private and responsible use of psychotropic plants.

It is the right of the person to decide whether or not to cultivate and ingest any plant on this earth of their choosing. Any plant that falls under the category of psychotropic is still permissible but its use must adhere to certain guidelines since they have the ability to temporarily alter perception, consciousness, mood or feeling, and public safety must be maintained. These guidelines can be decided by individual states but the recommended restrictions are as follows:

It is lawful to grow, possess and ingest any psychotropic plant as long as the person responsible for growing, possessing and those involved in consumption do not:

A) Cultivate more plants then is allowed for that specific type of psychotropic plant, unless a commercial license or augmented private license has been obtained.
B) Exchange any part of a psychotropic plant for money or goods without the proper commercial licensing.
C) Obtain or distribute any part of a psychotropic plant to a minor, unless you are the legal guardian of the minor.

Summery:

Basically what all that amounts to is that you can grow and possess any psychotropic plant as long as you don't go over the private limit. If you go over the limit then you are considered a commercial grower, and growing commercially without the proper license is illegal and a punishable offense. If you wish to grow an amount for private use that exceeds the limit then approval must be obtained and a tax must be paid for an expanded private license. You can give away psychotropic plants or fruit to friends and family, but you cannot accept money or goods for them, doing so would make you a commercial distributor of psychotropic plants, which is illegal without a license. You cannot grow, buy or distribute for or to a minor unless you are that minor's legal guardian.

Principle 2: Require state licensing for the commercial growing and distribution of psychotropic plants.

It is the right of the person to enter into the business of cultivating and/or distributing psychotropic plants for profit, providing that they adhere to certain guidelines since psychotropic plants have the ability to temporarily alter perception, consciousness, mood or feeling, and public safety must be maintained. Those guidelines can be decided by individual states but the recommended restrictions are as follows:

It is lawful to commercially grow, possess and distribute any psychotropic plant or plant parts as long as the person responsible for growing, possessing and distributing does not:

A) Grow, possess and distribute more plants then what is allowed for under the commercial license that has been acquired.
B) Distribute any chemically altered psychotropic plant or parts of psychotropic plants including ones that no longer appear in their natural form.
C) Distribute any psychotropic plant or parts of psychotropic plants to a minor.

Summery:

You can grow any amount of psychotropic plants exceeding what is allowed for personal use as long as you obtain the proper licenses beforehand. Licenses are sold regarding what psychotropic plant you want to grow and the quantity you intend on growing. Licenses also range from wholesale distributing by a large-scale grower to small shops selling just limited selection of psychotropic fruits. It is illegal to sell any psychotropic plant or plant parts that have undergone chemical changes or no longer appear in their natural form. The dehydration or drying of psychotropic fruits is permissible since it does not alter the chemical content of the plant and allows them to maintain their natural form. The commercial or private sale of extracts would be illegal, but if you make the extracts at home for personal use or if you give them to friends and family, then that is legal as long as you do not obtain money or goods for the psychoactive product. As it is with alcohol, it would be illegal for any commercial distributor to sell psychotropic plants or products to a minor.

Principle 3: Prevent distribution of psychotropic plants to minors.

It is the right of the person to decide whether or not to cultivate and ingest any psychotropic plant, unless such person is a minor. Since psychotropic plants have the ability to temporarily alter perception, consciousness, mood or feeling, one must be of legal age to participate in such activities. Those guidelines can be decided by individual states but the recommended restrictions are as follows:

It is unlawful to grow, possess and ingest any psychotropic plant if one is a minor unless:

A) You are the minor's legal guardian and privately administer such plants yourself.
B) You are a religious institute with the permission of the legal guardian and then only if the child is aware that they will be ingesting perception and behavior altering plants.

Summery:

Minor's are held to the same rules as with alcohol except that the age limit is 18 and also with the exception of it being the parents' determination if their child is to ingest psychotropic plants. If a parent does allow their child to consume psychoactive substances then they must administer them privately. Public intoxication of minors with or without parental consent is not tolerated and is illegal. It is already a common practice for religious institutes to administer psychoactive sacraments to children. Native American churches already have legal authority to give Peyote to its members and children. Catholic churches have also been giving Wine to children during communion for hundreds of years. So the second law is somewhat already pre-existing in today's society.

Principle 4: Prevent public intoxication and maintain driving restrictions.

It is the right of the person to decide whether or not to ingest any psychotropic plant but its use must adhere to certain guidelines since they have the ability to temporarily alter perception, consciousness, mood or feeling, and public safety must be maintained. These guidelines can be decided by individual states but the recommended restrictions are as follows:

It is lawful to ingest any psychotropic plant or psychoactive substance unless:

A) You do so in public view and exhibit public intoxication in non-designated areas.
B) Drive a vehicle or operate heavy machinery while intoxicated.
C) Fail to obtain proper licensing for a public establishment that allows the consumption of psychotropic plants.

Summery:

These laws almost fully mimic current alcohol laws. You cannot ingest psychotropic plants or exhibit intoxication anywhere in public unless it is designated for such use. Legal consumption places may be Marijuana smoking shops, some entertainment venues, and religious churches; very few of these plants will be consumed in public legally. If an establishment fails to obtain the proper licensing but still allows the public to ingest psychotropic plants there, then they will be prosecuted and punished.

Principle 5: Maintain the illegal status only on distributing synthetic psychoactive drugs for profit.

It is the right of the person to decide whether or not to grow and ingest psychotropic plants. It is also the right of the person to decide whether or not to make and ingest psychoactive drugs in private. However, it is illegal to distribute psychoactive drugs and changed forms of psychotropic plants for profit. These unnatural forms are considered illegal drugs and profiting off their distribution is an illegal activity punishable by law. Those punishments can be decided by individual states, substances that are not allowed for commercial distribution are defined below:

It is unlawful to distribute for profit an illegal drug, which can be defined as:

A) Any psychotropic plant that has been altered chemically or no longer appears in its natural form.

B) Any synthetic psychoactive substance that has not been approved by the Food and Drug Administration.

71

Summery:

This law follows the philosophy that we have a right to psychotropic plants, we have a right to do what we want with those plants, but if we alter them for any reason other than for personal use and distribute them or any other drug for profit, then that is illegal. One could still give away homemade psychoactive substances to friends and family as long as they do not collect money for them or distribute them to the public.

CHAPTER 06: FURTHER DISCUSSIONS ON EVERYDAY IMPLICATIONS

Let us now examine my drug plan and see what the societal implications are and why the laws that I have devised, safeguard us against abuse while also freeing us from the burden of the Drug War. It's not difficult to imagine a society that has adopted a free plant philosophy such as the one I have laid out. Most societies were free plant societies before the advent of modern times took place around the late nineteenth century. Societies before ours didn't crumble at the knees because of psychotropic plants, in fact most of them were around a whole lot longer than our modern one. But the goal of our new free plant society is to end the War on Drugs and help prevent people from abusing and distributing drugs, while allowing for the free use of psychotropic plants so that these plants can financially contribute to society. So imagine with me our new plant tolerant society. We have secured the right to put anything in our bodies and we have back our right to plants. We can grow any psychotropic plant for private use and we can go to the store and buy the natural product of any of these plants and ingest it and experience the various euphoric effects. The law is written to protect society from harm, let's look at how it does that.

The government shouldn't care what we put in our bodies and it is not their role to tell us what we can and cannot ingest. We have reinstated our right to plants for one reason and one reason only, to stop the Drug War. So if a person grows and consumes psychotropic plants while obeying the law then that is great. But if a person also grows their allotment and then chemically alters them, turning them into something like Cocaine or Heroin for private use then that too should be allowed by law. As long as they are not distributing their synthetic drug for profit they are complying with the new drug law. Who cares if that person is putting a harmful substance into their body, it's not the government's job to prevent them from doing so. There are no laws against drinking gasoline, so ingesting any substance with similar or less destructive properties such as synthetic, chemical drugs should likewise not have criminal implications. It is legal as long as you make it privately and ingest it privately, abiding by the right to our body. But the sale and manufacturing to distribute these substances for profit should be heavily criminalized as it is today. The goal of the new drug plan is to rid the world of the drug market or the distribution of drugs for money, because that is where crime and violence develops. Whether illegal drugs are synthetic or psychotropic plants they currently are worth their weight in gold, especially some of the synthetic drugs, which are worth more than ten times their weight in gold, making for a very profitable business for those who deal these substances. The high price for these illegal substances is what propels the drug trade, take away the extremely high profitability cushion and you put drug dealers out of business. How we reduce the price is a key part of my plan. We already know that making psychotropic plants legal will end the underground demand for those substances. Now with synthetic drugs we obviously can't abolish them because that is what the Drug War has been trying to do for years and failing, but having them legally regulated is not the best answer either. That's because there is no reason to commercially regulate Heroin, Cocaine, Speed, Ecstasy or LSD when you make, Opium, Coca, mushrooms, Peyote and Marijuana commercially available to everyone. The use and profitability of synthetic drugs will diminish because of the new tolerance for psychotropic plants. However, we need to understand that a few people are going to put these synthetic drugs in their body anyway, so lets at least give them the opportunity to make the drugs themselves instead of supporting the illegal drug trade. Because after all we don't care if they put the stuff in their bodies, as long as they do it in private, which is what most drug users do anyway. Allowing people to make their own drugs from plants and the minor occurrences of abuse that would arise is no where near as damaging as the crime and violence which gets incited by the Drug War today.

The worst characteristic of Drugs has nothing to do with the fact that they make people high, it is instead that they are so deeply imbedded with crime and violence that is most detrimental to society. All drugs are married to crime and violence, even Marijuana. All divisions of drug activity are illegal, whether you sell them, buy them, use them, distribute them, grow or make them it is all criminal activity. So when you seek to ingest drugs you are made a criminal and are forced to deal with criminals to obtain the substances. Unfortunately these criminals who you have to deal with are not in the business of distributing euphoric substances to make people happy, they do it for the money and lots of money at that. It is very disheartening that a positive and upstanding individual who wishes to smoke a little herb has to now engage with the type of violent people who often sell drugs. To obtain some of this natural herb they may have to invite a dangerous and aggressive, gun toting, criminal into their happy, loving and peaceful home. Often the fear of robbery and murder are going through their minds as they obtain this delightful little herb that otherwise would be a joy to receive, but the days of free growing and ingesting your own plants are long gone, and instead have been replaced by this maddening scene of dangerous underground activity. It is the profitability of these substances that make the dealer underhanded and violently protective of his ability to make money. Currently anybody who wants to get into the drug distribution business has the potential to make unlimited money, it really just depends on how far up the chain they are willing to go. The degrees of involvement vary from local dealers to drug gangs and king pins all the way up to manufactures, drug lords and drug cartels. The last example in some countries have become so wealthy and organized, they actually compete against the local government for power and control through a vicious campaign of violence and assassinations. No matter your rank in the drug distribution ring, your participation is propelled only by the desire for personal profit. So even the small-time local dealer makes enough money off the substance he sells to render it worthwhile. There is a different level of violence involved in every stage of drug distribution. The small local dealer doesn't invoke a whole lot of violence but they often keep some sort of weapon on them in case someone tries to steal their money and drugs. A lot of times small dealers may try to distribute bunk drugs which then may launch a cycle of violent paybacks. Some dealers even give drugs on loan to smaller distributors, expecting payment after the drugs are sold. They often give time limits and when it's time for them to collect their money they become very aggressive about it. All these violent tendencies are perpetuated even on this small level. When you examine larger scale distribution it gets even worse. Most large inner cities have a poor community with a rather sophisticated drug distribution network. A lot of times there are different types of gangs that maintain the distribution channels. These gangs range from young, teenage, ethnic minorities to prominent upper-class businessmen. The gangs that consist of young minorities are exceedingly violent. Often drug-selling territories are staked out all over urban cities, and when members of rival gangs sell drugs in another's claimed territory it often leads to violent confrontations between the two gangs, leading to many deaths. Drug distribution is the centerpiece to their violent and criminal pursuits and for them it is worth fighting to control. Now as you go further into drug distribution it increasingly gets more organized and sophisticated. Drug cartels are the biggest facet of the market and are at war against each other but more so at war with the government. They possess the resources to have heads of state assassinated and prisons broken into. They are terrorists not in the religious fanatical sense, but instead inflict terror to preserve their profitability and position in the drug market. It is the illegalization of all drugs that make every single one of them extremely profitable today. To dissemble this vast hierarchy of violence that is associated with drug distribution you must make all drugs financially unprofitable to distribute. By doing so you end the seemingly endless supply of money available to the dealers and drug lords and effectively bring their business to a crashing halt. No money to be made, no violence to be had.

Violence and crime also stem from the drug abusers themselves as they are constantly forced to come up with large amounts of money to support their addiction, more often than not driving them to crime or sex acts for money. The vast majority of drug users want to do drugs legally, but the fact that they are illegal and cost so much is what contributes to the drug problem, even the junkies don't want to have to rob and steal in order to afford drugs. You don't see many drug abusers stealing so that they can save the money for their future, they're turning right back around and spending it on drugs. By making psychotropic plants legal you're ending the price gouge on illegal drugs and you're also giving people alternatives that are actually much better for the individual who seeks a buzz on something other than alcohol. You now may be wondering about the drugs that you can't make from plants like Speed and Ecstasy (MDMA) and how the freeing of psychotropic plants reduces their availability? You can find almost identical highs that these synthetic drugs create in psychotropic plants. The fact is once psychotropic plants are firmly reestablished in society, people's dependency and desire for synthetic drugs will all but diminish completely, therefore dissolving the underground drug trade and the reliance on synthetic drugs. There will still be a very small market for illegal synthetic drugs but their control will be much more manageable because of the new funds available and the shift of attention by law enforcement, from all illegal substances, to only the distribution of synthetic ones. Proper drug education starting from grade school will be a big factor in preventing the abuse of dangerous drugs.

Legalizing psychotropic plants may initially make the quantity of synthetic drugs available on the streets such as Heroin and Cocaine go up, but after a very short period of time the price of these substances will drastically decrease, making them barely even profitable. Most people who will potentially be doing these synthetic drugs now have a legal alternative to other substances that are almost free and much healthier because they are natural. Why would anyone spend $160 for one gram of Cocaine on the streets, when if they really want it they can just make it themselves from their own Coca Plants for around $3 a gram? One gram is about how much a Cocaine addict goes through in one day. The same can be said for Heroin, which on the streets cost even more than Cocaine. But 98% of people who want to catch a buzz on anything other than alcohol will ingest the plant and leave it at that. Psychotropic plants pack a lot of bang for their buck, but they also have a tendency to promote positive use. Anyone who grows their own psychotropic plant will indeed have to learn about the plant before they are successful at growing it, this will force them to educate themselves on the plant, the cultivation and its euphoric properties. Then after all that learning, turning the plant into an unnatural substance by adding harsh chemicals is going to be the last thing they want to do with the plant. If they just buy the end product in the store then they will be educated on the warning labels on the package itself. Educating people about psychotropic plants and promoting them as safe alternatives to synthetic drugs should be a major goal of the new drug plan.

Now what keeps someone from growing a large number of plants and manufacturing synthetic drugs to distribute is the restriction on plant quantity. The number of plants that a person can grow for private use is set up so that they can grow and make enough drugs for themselves and themselves only. For a person to make a quantity of synthetic drugs that is great enough for them to profit from would require growing an enormous number of plants. For Heroin they would have to grow somewhere around at least 2-3 acres of Poppy flowers and for Cocaine they would have to grow more than 100 bushes. These are very inefficient plants to make drugs from unless you have thousands of acres in the right climate. If you think you can make drugs profitable by buying the psychotropic plant product from the store and then altering it yourself, think again. The taxes on the natural products and fruits of psychotropic plants will cause them to possess a fairly high price. Therefore it would not be efficient for a person intent on selling synthetic drugs to go into a store and buy 50 pounds of Coca leaves so he can turn them into Cocaine for street dealing. And if they try to buy them wholesale from a licensed grower, then a bulk purchasing licenses would be required and a wholesaler cannot distribute psychotropic products to an unauthorized receiver. The chances of people producing drugs from legal psychotropic plants and selling them will diminish once the drug market becomes unprofitable.

The exact number of psychotropic plants that people are allowed to grow privately is somewhat meaningless, if they go over the limit or even double it, it is not a huge deal. You just want to discourage people from growing acres of the plants so as to maintain the commercial cultivating regulations and prevent people from growing enough plants to make synthetic drug distribution profitable. Giving people reasonable psychotropic plant quantities to possess in private is fundamental to the new drug plan. Each psychotropic plant would have a different quantity and growing tolerance based on the individual characteristics of that plant. For the Marijuana plant it would be reasonable to allow the private growing of about 25 plants. This only includes mature Marijuana plants and not seedlings or cuttings that are under a month old. However, the cultivation limits on something like psychotropic mushrooms should be based on growing area. That is because plant quantity is not applicable since mushrooms grow from a large underground mycelium network and produce varying numbers of fruits. For the private grower,

100 square feet of inoculated growing area should be plenty sufficient, that is a 10' x 10' mushroom garden. Random outdoor patches in a large area are fine as long as their total volume is less than 100 square feet. The Opium Poppy flower could have a quantity limit of about 35 plants. This would not include small plants that are less than three inches because it is common to sow many seeds and then thin out the quantity after the sprouts have successfully grown. If all the seeds turn into sprouts then you still have to thin them out because Opium Poppy flowers need to have a certain distance between one another or the confined quarters will hamper their growth. The Coca plant could have a private limit of about 30 plants, whereas the growing limits on the Peyote cactus should be more around 100. That's because Peyote takes over ten years to mature, so for an individual to fulfill their private demand they would have to have many cacti in various stages of growth. Grafting the Peyote cactus helps get around this lengthy maturing process but the quantity should still be high because one person may consume up to 12 buttons at one time, and do so several times a year.

The amount of psychotropic fruits or natural plant products that one keeps in the privacy of their own home should not be regulated. There are several reasons for this, first the obvious reason corresponds to our current alcohol laws. There is no limit on the quantity of alcohol you can possess, people often keep much more alcohol on hand than they could possible drink in one night or even in one week, an example of that is the keeping of wine cellars. But the main reason for just regulating active growing psychotropic plants and not the quantity of psychotropic fruits or products is because it is unnecessary as long as all the other laws on psychotropic plants are intact. People should have the right to collect as many psychotropic fruits or products that they desire as long as they obtained them through legal means and do not distribute them for profit. Whether someone builds up a surplus by either growing their batch of psychotropic plants and harvesting them several times a year, or by commercially purchasing large quantities from the store, they will be very limited on what they can do with the products if they do decide to distribute them illegally. First of all if they grew psychotropic plants themselves to obtain the end products, they would not be able to grow enough plants for them to make any kind of profit without it being suspicious. A large field of Poppy flowers or Coca plants is just too obvious to be easily concealed. If they try to grow them indoors in a large warehouse then they wouldn't be able to grow enough to make it profitable. The indoor growing area would have to be close to the size of two football fields. It's just not economical to grow that many plants indoors so you can then turn it into Heroin or Cocaine for street sale. Now if someone goes the other route and buys their natural psychotropic plant products from the store and then alters them into a synthetic drug for street sale, it will be too costly of a process since the products in the store are highly taxed therefore giving them a high price. I'll remind you that even if someone does manage to get away with making a lot of synthetic drugs, there won't be a market for those substances since anyone can make their own basically for free. All licensed commercial growers would have regulations on how much they can grow and where they can sell it, and all the transactions would be closely monitored. So only active growing plants need to be regulated, you don't want fields of unregulated psychotropic plants everywhere or at least until America no longer has a synthetic drug problem.

Let's now examine why it is so important to only allow the commercial distribution of psychotropic plant products in their natural and unchanged form. Why can't we for example, allow the commercial sale of Hashish, which is in fact Marijuana in a chemically unchanged form, it is altered from its natural appearance but it has no chemical additives. Hashish is very innocent and you would think that its distribution wouldn't have any detrimental effects on society. It's not Hashish itself that is bad, it is allowing changed forms of psychotropic plants that negates the law. If you allow concentrations or extracts then you have no grounds to disallow Cocaine from being sold commercially. Hashish is just a more potent concentration of Marijuana's active alkaloid THC. Well that's what Cocaine is, just a concentration of one of the active alkaloids in the Coca Plant. Allowing the sale of unnatural forms of psychotropic products opens up the door for commercially distributing drugs and not plants. With this new drug policy, people would be fully allowed by law to make their own Hashish at home or even Cocaine for that matter, and give it to friends if their friends are willing to accept it, but they can't sell it and they can't buy it from the store. Keeping this law intact safeguards society from being the propagator of drugs. I imagine that the making of Hashish at home will be a widespread practice, and giving friends and family homemade Hash could be as common as giving them fruitcake during the holidays. Substances like Cocaine would not be a very welcomed gift among most people though.

I have made the recommendation in my drug plan that the legal age for participating in psychotropic plant activities is 18 instead of 21. You may think the reason for this lower age limit is since teenagers and young adults are the ones who currently use illegal substances the most, we should just cave in and allow them access to psychotropic plants earlier because they will obtain them anyway. But that is not my motive. At 18 you are legally an adult, you can go to war if you have to, you can legally sign contracts, buy pornography, or go to prison for criminal activity. There are many rights that come with being an adult in our society. By the age of 18 you can decide for yourself what religious persuasion you wish to believe without parental intervention. It just so happens that most psychotropic plants, if not all of them, have lots of evidence throughout history as being religious sacraments. The two most common religiously used North American psychotropic plants is the Peyote cactus and Psilocybe mushrooms. If a pre-eighteen year old wishes to pursue a belief that holds these plants to be sacred or wishes to gain spiritual enlightenment from them, but the parents of the child chooses to forbid their use, then that is the right of the parents. But when that child becomes an adult at the legal age of 18 and parents have no legal authority over him, he should have the right to grow and ingest psychotropic plants for whatever reason he chooses. People who are familiar with these plants know that almost all of them are much less addictive than tobacco and not quite as debilitating as alcohol. Combine that together with the possibilities of religious use and these plants should be available for those who are 18 or older.

It should be obvious that even though parents have a right to administer psychotropic plants to their children in private, child endangerment is not tolerated and as always it is a criminal offense. Parents are responsible for keeping their children out of harms way. Leaving psychotropic plants in easily accessible areas for children to find, is just as irresponsible as leaving a gun, harmful cleaning solutions or even alcohol in accessible places. They all could have very harmful outcomes if a child stumbles upon them, setting the parents up for possible prosecution. Also if a parent manufactures their own chemical drugs and exposes their children to an unsafe lab or toxic fumes, they can be prosecuted for child endangerment. It is more than likely that friends and family will be the ones alerting the authorities on this willful endangerment. Likewise the parent can also be prosecuted if they give their child any type of psychoactive substance and the child is either too young to understand the substance and has a negative reaction or if the parent allows the child to consume a large quantity possibly leading to an overdose. Any parent that has to take their child to the emergency room after ingesting psychoactive substances will more than likely be taking a trip to the police station afterwards. If a neighbor happens to notice that the kids next door are running around the yard exhibiting characteristics of someone highly intoxicated, then they may indeed call child services to come and check out the situation. Depending on the decision of child services, the parents may face fines or punishments. Usually if a young child between the ages of six and ten happens to ingest a small to moderate amount of a particular psychotropic plant they will have no permanent damages. They couldn't really consume enough Marijuana to be adversely affected by it. Eating small amounts of Opium will also only cause minimal effects. In fact many Eastern and Middle Eastern cultures add small amounts of Opium to their infants formula to help ease the pain of developing new teeth. However a substantial amount of Opium will have drastic effects on young children. Ingesting a small to moderate amount of psychotropic mushrooms will only cause a child to have a very strange and confusing experience leading to many questions once it is over, but accidentally ingesting a larger quantity of mushrooms may affect their mental development. Peyote is less of a concern since a child would have to eat a whole button or two to experience its effects and that is unlikely due to the unpleasant taste of the cactus. If they do happen to get a hold of some Peyote tea then its consequences will be the same as psychotropic mushrooms if a large amount is consumed. There are no grave effects if a child consumes small to moderate amounts of Coca leaves or Coca tea. Consuming larger amounts will inflict the same effects as if a child were to consume large amounts of Caffeine. Including irritability, nervousness, sleeplessness, and rapid heartbeat. Substantial quantities of either Coca or Caffeine could however have severe health affects on a young person. Children at young ages should not be ingesting psychotropic plants unless it is for medicinal reasons and then only in small quantities. Even under the terms of religious use children do not have the capacity to benefit from these plants until they are between the ages of 12 and 16 and then only if they have a full understanding of psychotropic plants. All children develop at different speeds so it is really up to the parents to monitor and decide when and if their children can consume psychotropic plants. But just as always parents are legally responsible for the safety of their kids.

We need to now examine what is encompassed in the term private use so that we can fully understand its impact in the free plant society. There may be some concerns regarding public distribution that we will look at also. Embracing this new drug plan in order to end the Drug War would require the removal of the legal penalties on the act of privately growing and consuming psychoactive substances. This would effectively allow people to grow any psychotropic plant and consume that plant in any way, or manufacture a psychoactive chemical substance and consume it. And it is legal as long as it is done in private or in a place sanctioned for its use. Private use is already a well-defined term in society, it basically means oneself and their friends and family, which effectively secludes the public from participating. Let's look at some examples of private and public use. It would be legal to have a private party with friends and family and consume psychoactive substances. A large party perhaps at someone's mansion where guests can consume psychoactive substances would also be legal as long as there was a specific guest list and the public was prevented from attending. At these private events one could give away psychoactive substances whether they are a plant or a chemical. However it would be illegal to give away psychoactive chemical substances or psychotropic plants to the public. Therefore someone could not stand on a corner and hand out free drugs or psychotropic plants to the public. In a public entertainment venue such as a music concert, it would also be illegal to give away free psychotropic plants during the concert. The venue could obtain the proper licensing to allow for the sale and consumption of psychotropic plants at the event, but since tickets are available to the public it would be illegal to give away free psychotropic plant products to anyone at the show. Synthetic substances would not be permitted in any form at public venues. Another area were the lines between public and private use needs to be defined is under the tolerance of religious use. Obviously the law would allow for the religious use of psychotropic plants, and a church that holds these plants to be sacred has the right to use them and administer them to its members. Let's simply call them "plant churches." The opposite of a plant church would then be a "chemical church." Since people have a right to ingest what they want, if a group holds a chemical substance to be sacred and wishes to start a religious church, they can do so but it would be a non-sanctioned church. Meaning the public could attend the church, but the church cannot give away synthetic drugs to the public or allow them to consume the drugs on church property. Religious synthetic drug participation would only be lawful if it is held by an individual on his or her own private property among family and friends, this could also include members of the church, but not the public. Basically how that translates is that you can have a church that allows the public to attend regular services where the church preaches and teaches about the experience and spirituality. But the actually drug sessions would be held on private property where only members could attend. Becoming a member would be a fairly tedious process like it is with any church. All the new laws regarding our right to ingest psychoactive substances will take into account these situations and prevent chemical drug distribution to the public in any form.

There are many issues regarding the legalization of psychotropic plants and it may bring up reservations for some, but the more you examine the possibilities, the clearer the whole picture becomes and the more attractive the idea is.

CHAPTER 07: COMMERCIAL AVAILABILITY & TAXES

If we choose to embrace this new drug plan then everyone will have the right to grow psychotropic plants for private use. It is our right as humans and it is the foundation that will lead to the end of the Drug War. But it is up to individual states to decide as to what extent they will tolerate the commercial sale of psychotropic plants and their natural products. Some states may see it fit to only allow their citizens the private growing and ingesting of these plants and that is fine, as that is the prerogative of that state's government and the people who live there and vote. Other states might only allow the commercial sale of psychotropic seeds and chose not to have psychotropic plants and natural plant products available commercially to the public. Then there will be states that not only allow the private growing and consuming of these plants but also permit the plants and their natural products to be sold commercially in dedicated shops to the public. They may also have public places and facilities available where one could ingest these plants legally and enjoy various forms of entertainment, not much different from today's alcohol bars. Some states may wish to only have Marijuana commercially available though. There are many options concerning the different degrees of availability and it is really up to the individual state and the people who vote there to decide how intermingled they want these plants with their community.

What needs to be realized though is the more open, widespread and accepted these plants are, the less profitable the synthetic, underground drug market becomes. The full commercial sale of psychotropic plants and their natural plant products will also allow those who seek intoxication to have natural alternatives to synthetic drugs. They won't head out on the streets looking for synthetic drugs and risk punishment for breaking the law when they have equally powerful substances available at the local psychotropic plant store. Likewise synthetic drug dealers won't engage in the illegal activity of selling synthetic drugs on the streets because their customer base will be decreased to almost nothing. Even if drug dealers do find a few people who will buy their drugs, they will not be able to sell them at the current inflated prices, because people can now just make their own drugs a whole lot cheaper or find a natural commercially available high that gives about the same effects without the illegal activity. This subsequently makes the underground market unprofitable. What may also occur if some states sell natural psychotropic plant products and others don't, will be people crossing the border of their non-commercial state into a commercial state and buying large amounts of psychotropic products and then selling them for profit back home in their community without a commercial distribution license. It will also lead to a market that is conducive to people growing psychotropic plants at home and then selling the natural products to their community, without the proper licensing. Therefore it is highly recommended that we integrate psychotropic plants and their natural products everywhere, it is the only method to completely stomp out underground distribution and synthetic drugs.

What is also important to commercial availability is the tax structure that we impose on these plants and their natural plant products. Since these are substances that can result in temporary changes in perception, consciousness, mood or feeling it is important that the government recovers a good amount of money from their use, so as to maintain proper control on them and keep up public safety as well as bring in additional income that can be spent on other public needs. If, for example, it eventually becomes the desire of one-third of the population to indulge in these plants responsibly, then let's make them also pay high taxes on these plants so that with taxes and all the money that's saved from ending the War on Drugs, the government will be overwhelmed with funds that will then lead to a better life for all citizens. Taxes are only collected on commercially grown or sold psychotropic plants and their natural products. The government will not seek compensation or licensing if you grow your own personal number of plants and do so in the privacy of your home. It is only when you seek to grow more plants than is allowed under private use that you will have to pay a tax to obtain the proper augmented private license. Other taxable activities also include purchasing plants or natural plant products from a commercial distributor or if you are a commercial cultivator or distributor yourself.

First the commercial availability starts with the growing of psychotropic plants, whether they're being cultivated locally or imported their proper regulation is imperative. A local commercial grower or cultivator is really nothing more than a psychotropic farmer. They have either devoted a large amount of land or a climate controlled green house to producing psychotropic plants. What makes them a commercial grower is the number of plants they produce, which can be defined as any amount over the quantity that is allowed for private use. Commercial growers will usually have many acres or thousands of square feet devoted to their psychotropic crops. There will also be small-scale garden nurseries that grow psychotropic plants. What these commercial growers have in common is that they will all be required to have a license to grow these plants and they will have to pay a tax or a fee every year to obtain that commercial cultivation license. The cost of that license depends on several factors. How many plants do they produce in a year, what plants are they growing, how large is their growing area, are they growing and selling just the plants or are they growing the plants in order to sell the natural plant products, including seeds, fruits, flowers or leaves. And are they distributing their plants and or natural plant products to a wholesale distributor or are they selling directly to the public.

A licensed cultivator will have certain provisions in his license that will determine whether he can sell plants and or natural plant products to a wholesale distributor or to the public. If the cultivator can sell to a wholesale distributor then they can offer their plants and natural products at bulk discounts plus the accompanying tax, but if the cultivator can also sell to the public then bulk discounts are not available to the public who then must pay regular prices and taxes. This is to prevent a citizen from being able to buy bulk plant products at cheap prices. For example, you wouldn't want someone to buy 100 pounds of Opium at a cheap bulk price so they can then turn it into ten pounds of Heroin and be able to make a profit from it on the streets. They can still buy 100 pounds of Opium at the normal public price and taxation but it will cost them a whole lot, making it inefficient and unprofitable for street sale. Under the limit for private growing, they would not be able to grow anywhere near the amount of Opium Poppies it takes to produce ten pounds of Heroin. A Wholesaler must have the proper licensing to purchase from a cultivator. An individual could not just approach a licensed grower and say I am a wholesaler and then purchase cheap bulk Opium. The grower would risk losing their license and possible legal punishment if they sold to those who are not permitted to receive bulk psychotropic plants and natural plant products. Even if someone does manage to get cheap bulk Opium and then turned it into Heroin, they wouldn't have the underground market anymore to sell it in and even if they found a few to buy it, no one would pay that much for it because they can just make their own.

The importation of psychotropic plants and their natural products are very easy to regulate. Plants coming into America that are grown elsewhere will allow us to help support the farmers in other countries, it will be a complete role reversal. Right now you have a large population of farmers in Afghanistan who grow the Opium Poppy. They depend on this crop for their livelihood, it provides for their entire family and is really one of the only type of plants that is conducive to grow in the area. It's a more profitable crop then say wheat and although the farmer never sees the quantity of money that the Opium goes on to make after the drug lords turn it into Heroin, they still make a moderate amount of money per harvest. The farmers aren't a part of the drug market, they just grow a plant that they have been growing for generations, and it's the aftermarket sale of it that turns it into dangerous drugs for the underground market. Unfortunately the U.S. government punishes the farmers by eradicating their crops with chemicals dropped from the sky by military planes. The government won't bother introducing new crops to these farmers or supplementing them financially for their losses. The same goes for the Coca Plant growers in South America; the U.S. government is intent on punishing the farmers since they can't control the drug lords. With the re-legalization of these types of plants, these farmers can continue to support their families with the only crop they know how to grow. America and other countries will import plants as well as the leaves, seeds and fruit for sale to the psychotropic consumer. When we do import psychotropic plants and their natural products they will be subject to taxes just as if they were grown locally. There will no longer exist the need to smuggle any natural psychotropic plant products over the border because it would now be a legal industry. And even if smuggling something like raw Opium over the border does happen just to avoid paying taxes, it will be a rare occasion and have as little of an impact as smuggling cigarettes currently does. You really never see people or stores pushing untaxed cigarettes, this is because the amount of money you make on them without paying taxes is relatively small since tobacco is a legal product. Smuggling illegal synthetic drugs over the border will become equally as rare because the market and high prices of drugs will be almost completely eliminated by the arrival of legal psychotropic plants. It is my estimation though that most psychotropic plants that a country consumes will be grown locally since these plants are all easily grown indoors and most of them can be grown outdoors in a variety of climates as well.

The tax structure could really be anything on these plants and their natural products, all it needs to do is bring in a lot of money for the government. In my opinion the tax structure should consist of a three-level hierarchy, what I mean is that there should be varying tax levels for the different natural psychotropic products. The first tax level would be the lowest, maybe a tax on the final retail product of about 5% or so; this smallest tax would solely be for the sale of psychotropic seeds. It would be the philosophy of the government to promote the private growing of these plants at home, because when people grow them at home they become better educated about the plants. Therefore the low tax on seeds would reflect that. The second tax level would be for the sale of psychotropic plants and would maybe have a final retail tax of around 10%. The plants would be defined as any degree of growth from sprouts to mature plants. The third and final tax level would represent the highest tax and would be applied to all natural psychotropic products that are in their final natural form and ready for consumption. Examples of these would be the

Marijuana flowering tops, Psilocybe mushrooms, raw Opium and Coca leaves. Really anything that is in its natural and final form and ready to ingest right out of the package would be subject to about a 20% tax on the final retail product. The tax scheme could also include pre-consumer taxes such as ones that are applied to wholesale distribution according to volume or weight of the product. Tax implications on psychotropic plants and their natural products are unlimited and the revenue that they could bring in for the government could be enormous. Complimentary to these taxes are the licenses that are required for all commercial growers and distributors of psychotropic plants. There needs to be a wide variety of licenses that are available for the different levels of psychotropic plant participation. One who grows large amounts of psychotropic plants would be required to register with the state, purchase the appropriate license and then only distribute to licensed sellers or wholesalers. Selling directly to the public would require an additional license.

It is important to consider the commercial form of psychotropic plants and their natural products when being sold to the public. How will they be packaged, who will sell them, what kind of prices can we expect and how do we maintain their safe distribution? These are all key questions regarding the commercial availability of psychotropic plants, and it is imperative that they are distributed in a safe and regulated manner that promotes education. Failing to do so will not dissolve the synthetic drug market and will ultimately lead to more junkies and unsafe psychotropic plant use.

Let's examine the many safe and effective ways to distribute these plants and their natural products. First and least complicated is the distribution of psychotropic plant seeds. Seeds will carry the minimal tax and be sold in garden supply stores as well as being available through mail order and other outlets. In the stores they will be in a dedicated area that prevents minors from gaining access to them. Secondly we'll consider the selling of live plants. Some licensed cultivators will grow psychotropic plants not for the fruit or natural product but for the plant itself. They will ship the plants in various stages of growth to a public distributor, or basically a psychotropic plant store. One could walk into the store and see many rows of different types of psychotropic plants all in various stages of growth, from sprouts and young plants all the way up to mature plants that are getting ready to fruit. The prices on these plants would be equated to their stage of growth, obviously a mature plant is going to cost a lot more then a young one of the same species. So you pick out the plant you want according to cost or how far along it is in its developmental stage. You take it up to the counter, they will give you an informational packet like they do with most common plants sold today that contains care and maybe even consumption instructions. The clerk rings up the plant, the cost includes the 10% tax. The tax on this transaction is of the second level and therefore lower than if you were to just buy the psychotropic product itself, because now you have to take the plant home, develop it further and possibly fruit it before you can ingest the final psychotropic product. Really the commercial sale of psychotropic plants would be no different from buying a tomato plant, except that you will be paying certain additional taxes and the plants fall under established restrictions that prevent them from being sold to minors and so forth. There will be a range of psychotropic garden stores that sell these plants, from small shops that sell a very limited selection of plants to large nurseries that grow their own plants, harvest their own natural products, and sell varying degrees of both. The proper license will allow them to do so. When selling psychotropic plants they need to have clear labeling and reside in a dedicated area that is enclosed with a dedicated clerk so as to prevent minors from gaining access to psychotropic plants and thieving or eating them. You will also have large farms that permit the public onto their property to choose the best plant from a large selection of plants. It will almost be identical to the farms you have today that allow people to cut down their own Christmas tree or pick their own pumpkin or fruit tree, except that they will be picking their own psychotropic plants. Likewise there will be farms that when their psychotropic crop is mature will allow people to harvest their own psychotropic plant product or fruit, just like some farms allow you to pick your own oranges, cherries or corn and so forth. When they have chosen their psychotropic plant or plant product they will pay for it upon leaving thus allowing the government to collect its taxes. Lastly is the commercial distribution of the natural psychotropic plant products, the end result, what people will be consuming in order to obtain the various euphoric effects. These products should not be sold on isles in a grocery store or on shelves at gas stations. They must be isolated from minors so that they cannot easily thieve them. The ideal place would be similar to a freestanding liquor store. It must be a place where a minor cannot easily enter and browse around. A minor going into a liquor store would receive immediate attention because all liquor stores have a dedicated clerk near the store entrance, if suspicion arises that a minor has entered the store, the clerk quickly asks for age verification. It is common knowledge among minors that liquor stores do not tolerate their presence nor do they offer their products to them, so minors rarely enter liquor stores. A psychotropic plant store should be just as exclusive. Obviously it would be unwise to mix psychotropic plants and products together with non-psychotropic products, plants that make people high must clearly be identifiable as psychotropic and secluded from all other products. For supermarkets or grocery stores it should be permissible to offer psychotropic products, so long as they are in a closed area with a dedicated clerk at the entrance to observe age.

Now that we've seen how psychotropic plants and their natural products can commercially be distributed, lets examine what form these natural products will take and how they will be made available for public consumption. It's pretty easy to imagine the future products, they will closely resemble today's model for doses and quantities. When a person goes to the psychotropic store they will be presented with a variety of quantities and package designs each one unique to the individual plant product. Each product packaging will include recommended dosage, and use instructions plus health and addiction warnings if applicable. The packaging and informational data will help teach the consumer, so that they can learn the proper handling and usage of the psychotropic plant product.

You'll see Marijuana being distributed in several forms. The sale of seeds, mature plants and young plant clones or cuttings will be extremely popular, but its biggest selling natural product will be the Marijuana flowering tops, the buds. They are dried then bagged and sold in quantities ranging from one-eighth of an ounce to multiple ounces. It is a smoking herb that will have widespread use and popularity much like tobacco and alcohol. It will require packaging with warning labels very similar to tobacco, but with the included disallowance warning on operating vehicles while under the influence. The packaging will include the amount of dried Marijuana in a sealed clear plastic bag or in cigarette pack-like box. There will be some kind of light cardboard cover or attachment and printed on it will be the immediate plant specifics including, plant species and strain, growth parameters and price of product. Also on the cardboard will be any immediate Surgeon General Warnings. There will be a foldout paper attachment with detailed recommendations. These recommendations will include various subjects such as consumption and usage. Recommended usage will include ideas such as audio or visual entertainment, socializing or meditation. Health warnings would suggest that vaporizing or eating Marijuana is the most harmless way of ingestion and long-term smoking can lead to cancer etc. The included data sheet should have an abundance of information on it regarding the specific psychotropic product. Marijuana plants will also include a product data sheet when purchased but it will have additional growing information as well.

The Opium Poppy is another psychotropic plant that will be distributed naturally in several forms. Seeds are and will always be very popular, and even though eating the poppy seed bagel is almost rampant, growing these flowers for beauty alone, which today is borderline illegal, will increase their popularity still. And of course growing the flower for consumption purposes will be very common too. Mature poppy flowers will be commercially available and hold a strong market with lots of generated taxes but won't sell as much as raw Opium sap, the end product. Opium is the sap from the poppy flower pod and if you remember it's exuded when you cut into the ripe poppy pod. The sap is dried and compressed into blocks, which is how it is distributed and smoked, except it will only be sold in small quantities. Opium sap will be distributed in chunks that resemble portions of a chocolate bar. It is distributed in compressed dry blocks of sap and you break off a chunk no bigger than half of a pencil eraser and smoke it in your pipe. When sold commercially the amount will comprise very small quantities of Opium and with the taxes, it will be the most expensive natural psychotropic plant product available. The high consumer cost of commercial Opium will encourage users to grow their own and it will also keep them constantly aware of their participation with this plant, leading to hopefully a more knowledgeable user who safeguards against addiction. Probably the smallest commercially packaged amounts would represent less than a dozen single doses. So if a single dose for a person who has no tolerance from regular use is roughly about the size of a match head, then a full match would comprise about eight highs. So picture a small chunk of dark brown raw Opium two inches long and a little thicker than a wooden match. It would have equal perforations all the way down indenting into it eight detachable squares. Single doses are easily measured and then broken off. It will come sealed in a plastic bag with a cardboard cover and all pertinent information labeled, including price and quantity of highs and amount by weight. Then also attached is the fold out psychotropic data information, including specifics and warnings. Of course you can buy larger quantities of Opium at some stores, they will vary in sizes from chocolate bars to a quarter of a bar and the more affordable one-eighth of a chocolate bar. It is still more cost efficient to grow your own poppies though, if the private limit was 35 plants then you could easily produce around an ounce and a half, that's a couple of chocolate bars of Opium every four months. That is a generous amount for someone plus their many friends and family, but it is not enough to supply a junkie with unlimited Heroin. Packaged Opium will have all the required details on their data sheet but since it the only physically addictive psychotropic plant product, it will have addiction and frequency of use warnings.

The Coca Plant will most commonly be distributed either in whole plant form or in bags of fresh or dried leaves and additionally there will also be a small market for Coca seeds. Buying and growing the plant itself will only be mildly popular because you need to mimic the conditions of its natural habitat, which is tropical and hot with lots of rainfall and not everyone will be willing to invest in a green house. So seeds and live plants will have a small minority of the market, but the Coca Leaves themselves will be extensively distributed. Dried Coca leaves will be distributed in tea form just like today's Caffeinated teas. It will be billed as tea that has stimulant properties that are very similar to coffee while quite possibility being less addictive than Caffeine or at the most equal to Caffeine. It is quite possible that after an initial waiting period has passed observing the successfulness of the legalization of plants, the government may move to reclassify the Coca plant, allowing Coca tea to be distributed along side coffee and Caffeinated tea in public cafes or restaurants. Psychotropic Coca tea bags will be sold in the psychotropic section of stores. Large bags of dried Coca leaves are available too but they will cost a decent amount because all Coca leaves are of the highest tax grouping. Most psychotropic plant stores will have a large refrigerator dedicated to fresh Coca Leaves. Inside will be bags full of fresh green Coca leaves with quantities ranging from one ounce to one pound. Chewing these leaves will become popular too for their health benefits, nutritional content and as a natural source of energy. The commercialization of the Coca plant could demonstrate to be extremely successful. The plant in its natural form has near zero harm on the person, so it exhibits a potential to benefit from commercialization only second to Marijuana. The governmental revenue from the Coca Plant alone will be enormous because Coca leaves are the final natural product, giving them the highest tax, and their potential for widespread use is probably not comparable to lettuce but maybe more so to spinach.

The distribution of Psychotropic Mushrooms will also take on several forms, the most common being dried and bagged mushrooms. However, fresh psychotropic mushrooms will be almost equally as popular and can be found in the refrigerated section of your local psychotropic plant store. Also proving to be very popular will be the home growing of psychotropic mushrooms. Watching these mushrooms grow is a fun and unique experience unlike that of any other psychotropic plant, because once the optimal conditions inside their growing chamber have been reached, they shoot up almost instantly in just a few days. Dried psychotropic mushrooms will be sold much like today in quantities of one-eighth an ounce up to a couple of ounces or so. Most people who want an ounce or more will be inclined to just grow their own since they cost a fair bit once you get up into higher quantities. Fresh mushrooms are unique and many people don't like the taste of dried ones, so there will develop a market for picking and growing your own fresh mushrooms. A lot of psychotropic plant stores will have a rotating crop of fresh mushrooms on hand. Fresh mushrooms once picked do not last more than 5-7 days unless completely dried, so it would be convenient to have different stages of crops growing, that would allow the seller to quickly replace the ones that have been sold and those that are getting old. Fresh mushrooms weigh a lot more than dried ones obviously but most mushrooms are also slightly more potent when eaten fresh as apposed to dry. Dried mushrooms have a much longer shelf life, up to two years. Fresh mushrooms can always be dried in order to preserve them, so if the fresh ones aren't selling right away, you'd just pick them and let them dry completely so you can at least sell them as dried mushrooms instead of wasting them. Some stores will have their fresh mushrooms pre-picked and bagged in the refrigerator while other stores will allow you to pick your own from their grow area, you'll then just place the fresh mushrooms in a bag, weigh them and pay for them. The sale of all mature mushrooms, dried or fresh, will have the highest tax since they are the final, natural, psychotropic plant product. For those who want to grow their own mushrooms at home they have basically two options. They can buy the psychotropic mushroom spores and grow from scratch or they can buy a pre-inoculated substrate kit. The seeds of mushrooms are actually called spores and all psychotropic spores are sold legally today in most of the United States, legal to buy and possess but not legal to grow. Most stores will have a wide selection of psychotropic mushroom spores as well as plenty of information and books on their cultivation. They will also have mushroom grow kits, which are an easy grow-at-home method and are currently legal for sale in some of Europe. Mushroom grow kits consist of nothing more than mushroom growing soil, which is technically called substrate, and the required nutrients in a tin pan that has been pre-seeded with Psilocybe spores. After a couple of weeks it will fruit psychotropic mushrooms under a clear small plastic dome. It's the easiest way to grow mushrooms without all the fuss but the kits will have a higher price since most of the workload is already done with minimal intervention. Therefore it may be cost effective just to grow your own from spores and homemade substrate. Psychotropic mushroom grow kits are of the second tax category because they have formed the underground mycelium network already, which is basically the mushrooms "root" system. So it is a live plant that has not fruited yet, the fruit being the mature mushrooms that spring forth from the mycelium. Spores are obviously under the tax category of seeds because they are the reproduction unit indicative to fungi.

Peyote will most likely be distributed as dried buttons or cactus tops, maybe in single packs and four packs. But the live Peyote plant will rival in popularity too because its cultivation is possible in many unique ways. Peyote seeds will have a moderate market but live plants will sell much better. The cactus takes a long time to mature in nature, over ten years, but with its versatile growth parameters it can easily be grafted onto other faster growing cacti and made to mature in about one year. It's a fascinating process of experimentation and regeneration. Commercializing the Peyote cactus would be very beneficial because with its lengthy maturing process and its confinement to the small region between Southwest North America and Central Mexico, its natural population is decreasing. Once legalized this cactus will experience a huge boom in use but it is most likely that it will be the least widespread out of all the new legal psychotropic plants. However, making it less difficult on the Native American community to obtain and use this cactus is worth freeing it for that reason alone because even though they can legally use Peyote, they still encounter some persecution by law enforcement for doing so.

Because the psychotropic plant industry requires strict oversight and regulations, the plants will always have a moderately high price. Let's speculate on possible reasonable prices for these substances and how its future legal price may compare to its current illegal price. Now keep in mind that a good portion of the overall consumer price will be collected as taxes. All prices are purposefully set to be somewhat expensive due to the high taxing so as to always promote the private growing of these plants and bring in enough money to maintain their proper regulation.

Under the new drug law, dried Marijuana will probably carry a price of about $40 for a half ounce of high-grade sinsemilla, which usually has been hydroponically grown. Currently today half an ounce of that same kind of weed goes for $200. There will probably be a smaller market for what now is called commercial or medium grade weed, which is better than what is normally called shwag or low-grade weed. It may have a future going price of $40 an ounce compared to its current street price of $80-120 an ounce. Low-grade Marijuana or brick bud will almost certainly become extinct. Normal mature Marijuana plants will probably have a going price of $40-60 each, but the ones that have been extensively bred and are high potency strains will fetch a somewhat higher price. Prices of plants will increase as the plant itself matures and flowers. Clones or cuttings represent the other side of the Marijuana plant market. Clones are not whole plants for sale but are just small branches cut off a highly prized mature Marijuana plant and are then nourished and grown into identical mature plants by the consumer. Marijuana clones will have an average price tag of $15-25. Seeds too will definitely be popular, especially the ones that have been crossbred to produce specific varieties and have also been feminized so to produce only female Marijuana plants. These top quality seeds already have a large international market today, their current commercial price is around $30 for 12 seeds. Their future availability under the new drug law may dictate these seeds drop to about a $1 each but not much less since they are highly prized designer seeds. The industrial version of the Marijuana seed is the Hemp seed, it comes from a very low potency variety of the Marijuana plant and valued only for non-ingestible commercial crops such as paper, wood and rope. Its seed in the future won't cost anything less because already today they're very inexpensive at only a few bucks for a pound of Hemp seeds.

The Coca Plant itself has a small commercial market today, it's the leaves and the Cocaine alkaloid that gets the vast distribution. We can eliminate the drug Cocaine from future commercial distribution; it will only exist among a small, private minority and have no significant profitability. In its place will emerge the sale and profitability of Coca Seeds, leaf and plant. The price when buying Coca seeds will be minimal because their growing is somewhat confined, for $10 you'll get about a dozen seeds. Coca plants that are grown and sold at garden nurseries or imported will, depending on age and size, cost between $75-200. It is no doubt that Coca leaves will have the biggest market though. You may see dried Coca leaves packaged in tea bags and used as frequently as coffee or Caffeinated tea, people will drink it for similar reasons too. A box of Coca tea will probably cost as much as a box of fine quality tea does today, which is about $5. If Coca tea gains approval to be distributed along side coffee and Caffeinated tea in public cafes or restaurants, then another market is opened, but the price of commercially brewed Coca tea will stay comparable to today's coffee prices. Of course dried Coca leaves will be sold in big bags for those who wish to brew at home. A commercial bag of dried leaves weighing one pound couldn't cost more than $16 I'd presume. Fresh Coca leaves have an impressive market too, I couldn't imagine a psychotropic plant store not stocking them because they are a healthy natural source of energy, which might attract a variety of people. Fresh leaves are heavier but you could probably pick up a pound of them for around $10.

Maintaining a high retail price on Opium is specifically designed to discourage addiction and encourage the private growing of the poppy. You could easily and relatively at zero cost privately grow 35 poppies to support your Opium habit. But if you want to commercially purchase your Opium then it will cost a good amount of money that in turn goes straight to improving your community through local taxes. Raw Opium will be mainly sold in small quantities to the public. We already established the 8-hit perforated stick that looks like a big matchstick; it would probably weigh 4-8 grams and have a consumer price of $25.

Bigger quantities of a few ounces and more will typically range up to a couple hundred dollars. Live Opium Poppy flowers will be sold singly in a pot; if it is a mature poppy with a rip pod for sale then it will probably cost $30-50. Sprouts or young poppy flowers will commonly be sold at a fairly low price maybe $5-10 each. Opium Poppy seeds are already one of the cheapest seeds on earth, which probably has a lot to do with the fact that so many seeds are in one pod. Thousands of seeds can come from collecting and drying one seedpod. Plus with the popularity of the poppy seed for food, it has become a very widespread seed making it cost very little. The seeds of certain varieties of the Opium Poppy may cost a bit more but this tiny seed will always hold prices in the range of $20 an ounce for fertile growing seeds and mere pennies an ounce for commercial food grade seeds. An ounce of poppy seeds is well over 30,000 seeds.

Dried and bagged psychotropic mushrooms are usually sold in weights of one-eighth of an ounce to several ounces and are almost always the Psilocybe Cubensis species of psychotropic mushrooms. Today's prices are between $150-200 an ounce. Under the new drug law a one ounce bag of dried mushrooms may cost about $80, making a half ounce bag $40. Fresh mushrooms will probably cost about the same as dried ones but you'll get fewer mushrooms since they do weight more. Other more difficult to grow Psilocybes, will cost a little more and dried Amanita Muscaria mushrooms will maintain their current price of $25-40 an ounce since they already are legal to distribute. Growing kits with precolonized substrate will range from $25-40 each. Its growing space takes up one square foot so if the private growing limit was set at 100 square feet, then you could have 100 of these grow kits blooming and still be in legal compliance. Spores are always available for those who want to grow their own mushrooms from scratch and they will pretty much have the same price as they do today since Psilocybe mushroom spores are commercially legal for non-growing purposes. That price is roughly $15-25 for an enormous amount of spores contained in either a syringe with water or a print of spores on paper, which is then archived inside a sterile plastic bag.

If we commercialized psychotropic plants then that is what their future could look like. All plants would be taxed, all natural products regulated, and all commercial cultivators and distributors would be licensed. Everything would be legal and in the open instead of illegal and wild in the underground market. You would mainly have farmers and the government profiting off these plants instead of the criminal drug lords. It would be a welcomed natural industry compared to the dangerous underground drug market that we have today. These are really the only two options available for our modern society. You can either have an underground, psychoactive substance market or a legal and viable psychotropic plant market. These markets cannot thrive simultaneously so you must choose one over the other, so far we have chosen the underground market over the legal psychotropic plant market. However, even though we already have an illegal drug market we are not destined to have one forever, because once a legal plant market is developed it can easily overcome the underground drug market. As you have seen, a psychotropic plant market can be implemented in a controlled manner. When legislation is thoughtfully devised and psychotropic plants are properly regulated, the possibilities of it having a negative impact on society are very minimal. Psychotropic plants have a lot of commercial potential. The taxes on these plants could provide the government with a large amount of new money. And ending the financial burden that is the Drug War could free up even more money. It is imperative that we commercialize these plants in a safe and effective manner, doing so will benefit society in more ways then can be imagined. But if we don't incorporate new education into society at the same time and we also fail to regulate psychotropic plants properly, then their commercialization could have regretful consequences. Realistically though, the job of managing the commercialization of psychotropic plants effectively, would be much less difficult then waging a yearly Drug War.

Chapter 08: Preventing Abuse By Promoting Education

Society cannot rely on parents to educate their children properly on drugs and that is because most parents know absolutely nothing about the illegal substances. Instead, the public education system must devise a fully effective course itself. So far public drug education is a complete failure and any previous success can be attributed to nothing more than luck or natural fluxation in the number of users.

It is the current prohibition climate that is responsible for the indifference that drug users have for their body and their over all well-being. With all drugs banned and the overall miseducation about drugs, current users don't know the differences between drugs and have no knowledge about alternative psychotropic plants. By legalizing these plants you send a powerful message to people that says: these are the natural substances that mankind has used throughout all time to alter their consciousness, we find them to be least harmful and they are free to use, it is up to you if you want to participate in them, if you do then we will hold you to their responsible use. The other side of that message says that these synthetic substances are worthless and harmful to your body but if you want to ingest them you will have to learn about them and make them yourself, as long as you do that we will not prosecute you. Along with the new availability of psychotropic plants comes a real education process. You can no longer propagate biased untruths about what drugs and psychotropic plants are and what effects they produce. One of the stranger compulsions of our current drug education program is its persistence in concealing the different types of non-alcohol highs that are produced by drugs. There is really no reason to lie to young people about what drugs and psychotropic plants do.

Drug miseducation has been going on for close to 100 years; it was a little worse and misleading back in the early twentieth century, but even now it is far from being accurate and helpful to those being educated. Because of all this lack of proper drug-related knowledge in society, there is a huge understanding gap between those who have experienced drugs and psychotropic plants and those who have not. It is they that do not have any drug experience who ineffectively designed our current drug prohibition system. Looking at out current model for drug education you can basically think of it this way: all you ever learned about drugs and drug use only applied to Heroin. They took the worst attributes of Heroin and applied them to all drugs right down to the softer drugs and plants. Even Marijuana was once billed as being so evil it grew from the devils nostrils and so addictive it was worth killing for. So you really never have been properly educated on anything less than Heroin, unless you've done an illegal drug yourself and know its effects.

The philosophy of modern drug education is that the youth cannot be trusted to decide for themselves if illegal drugs are harmful enough to stay away from. So drug educators instead exaggerate the harmful effects and give such minimal information describing the high so as not to intrigue the young impressionable kid into wanting to try it. That is essentially what is wrong with our current drug education program. First of all you cannot tell kids that all illegal substances are extremely harmful, they will disregard that advice the first time they smoke Marijuana or talk to someone who smokes Marijuana, and then they will question all their previous drug education. It is plainly obvious to any drug user and anyone with a little bit of knowledge on the subject, that some illegal substances are very harmful while others are relatively safe unless abused. Secondly there is no reason to hide the truth from people about what drugs do, that is what type of high or enjoyable experience is derived from ingesting the substance. Drug education should be plain as day and as honest as possible. The more accurate the drug education is, the more readily equipped the individual will be in deciding if they do or do not want to participate. Drug education should be very in depth. Right now educators try to influence your decision to abstain while you are still very young. It is usually around 11 or 12 years of age that children are first exposed to drug education. This early drug education can be summed up as nothing more than a quick flash of persuasion while you are still very young, usually involving two one-hour meetings a week for about a month, most commonly in the form of a D.A.R.E class or special speaker. Then it is usually supplemented with one health class that somewhat touches on drug use during your sophomore year of high school. Other than an occasional public broadcast message you may hear, that sums up the American drug education program. You will never have any more drug education unless you land yourself in rehab when you are older. What needs to be done instead is a long persistent and truthful drug-educating program. It shouldn't be too intense when children are still young, but at the age of 12 or 13 schools should begin a course of drug education by thoroughly describing drugs, psychotropic plants, positive use, negative abuse, growing and manufacturing, and include better education on alcohol and tobacco.

The first drug educating years around 12 and 13 should be dedicated to describing all substances that can make people high. This would include showing actual images and footage of psychotropic plants being grown, what they look like, and how they're cultivated. Then show the chemical process of turning plants into drugs, the entire process, showing how sulfuric acid and kerosene are added to crushed Coca leaves in order to extract the Cocaine alkaloid, plus all the other chemicals and steps involved in making Cocaine. Show Heroin being made, where it comes from, how it is used, and the real-life effects of it. Also show the real use and abuse of Marijuana. It is important to detail the good and the bad of every mind-altering substance. What should also be taught equally at this point is drug history, including the past Drug War, drug gangs, crime and what led to the legalization of psychotropic plants; all ancient religious use should also be taught or at least acknowledged. When kids are this young you still want to be a little vague on what highs these substances create, because trying to understand the different properties of intoxication is very difficult when you're young. It is even difficult today for adults who have never done a drug to understand the possible highs that are created. As kids get older and more able to comprehend the internal effects of drugs, that is when you teach them thoroughly on the subject of highs.

When kids are 14 and 15 you can start giving them more advanced drug education, which includes reiterating their earlier education and expanding on it more vividly while also starting to teach about the highs and the serious health effects that some drugs cause on the body. It is important that young people get their complete drug education by the age of 16. It is by that age that teenagers become fully equipped and resourceful enough to drastically abuse these substances, so education needs to be sustained as a deterrent from synthetic drug use, while also serving as preparation for when they're 18 or 21 and can legally use psychotropic plants, alcohol and tobacco. If you teach kids properly then they will choose not to ingest synthetic drugs and use psychotropic plants responsibly if they do seek to get high. Really for kids at this age, you could properly educated them on mind and body-altering substances, by showing them a series of three or four two hour long drug education movies. These movies would detail every aspect of drug and plant use while also serving as the type of visual media that kids these days learn best from.

If psychotropic plants were to be legalized, then the education process would manifest in two waves or two different forms over society. It is extremely important that everyone gains a full understanding of all these substances so abuse will be limited. The first wave is the public education or re-education process, which will consist of properly teaching the public and the voters about synthetic drugs and psychotropic plants. It will mainly be undertaken by the head legalization alliance, which also determines the best media outlets for the messages. It will take on the form of a political campaign that begins advertising many years before the actual election and it will be a direct and factually based program that extends its way through just about every media outlet there is. Taking advantage of all communications such as radio, TV, print, Internet, film and various promotional assemblies as the mediums for broadcasting psychotropic plant education and the choice to legalize them. It will be an expensive campaign but an informative one. The second new wave of education will be geared towards the youth as we initiate new drug education programs in the schools so they can be educated early on when it is most appropriate.

The entire goal of the new drug education program is to thoroughly educate the population, young and old, so that if they indeed had access to every psychotropic plant, and psychoactive chemical substance, they would have the knowledge to use the substance in a beneficial manner or have the sense to stay away from it. Of course most people will choose not to participate in the use of these substances, especially the more intense ones, but it is important that everyone receives proper drug education.

Once honest and detailed drug education has been thoroughly integrated into society, people will have a full understanding of the substances, and therefore will be able to judge for themselves their level of participation. With the proper education, people will know how harmful some synthetic drugs are and choose to abstain from those substances, but if they are inclined to experience that type of high then they will know where to go in the plant world to obtain those effects naturally. People will understand that there is an equally powerful but much safer psychotropic plant for every synthetic drug. And so the majority of today's synthetic drug users will naturally shift to psychotropic plants for their altering experiences, once they become legally available and accepted. Knowing which plants will replace what drugs takes some knowledge and experience in the field of illegal substances. Let's now examine these shifts.

We know Marijuana is very popular as well as completely safe if vaporized or eaten and it will always be the most widely used psychotropic plant, but what drug could Marijuana replace while delivering an equally satisfying effect if we legalize it? The answer to that is easy alcohol. Even though alcohol is not illegal it is by far the most abused substance. It takes a devastating toll on society when misused, quite often with violence and death being the outcome. Alcohol is a substance that one can easily overdose from, which usually leads to alcohol poisoning and even death. Plus it is prone to cause addiction and dependency resulting in alcoholism. Drinking heavily for 20 years will more than likely give you cirrhosis of the liver or many other alcohol-related health problems. On top of all that it has an extremely negative impact on people already suffering from depression. Frequently these people will be more likely to attempt suicide if they abuse alcohol while suffering from depression. Alcohol is a substance that can all too easily become harmful and dangerous to society and the individual. Marijuana on the other hand, creating a very elated experience, does the exact opposite of alcohol while still allowing people that release after a long hard day at work. It causes very little harm to society and if it was legal it would cause even less. It is nearly impossible to overdose on Marijuana, you couldn't inhale enough to overdose on and your stomach would not be able to contain the amount it physically takes to overdose. You can possibility get a little sick from smoking too much at once, but that has more to do with the amount of toxins you're inhaling because of the smoke than it does with what is actually in the Marijuana. If you vaporize or eat your Marijuana it becomes an almost completely safe method of intoxication. Vaporizing it several times a week for 20 years will in no way inflict the health problems that heavy alcohol drinkers get during the same period of time. It is not physically addictive at all and has a tremendous ability to ease and maybe even cure depression. Marijuana in a free-plant society should be encouraged as a replacement for alcohol or at least as a subsidiary so people use alcohol half as much.

The psychotropic Coca Plant could easily replace Cocaine, and Speed. These two drugs are really just hyper energy drugs, and since they are both made unnaturally and contain additional harmful chemicals, the knowledgeable user will seek to replace their high with a less chemical one. Chewing plain Coca leaves will give an increase in energy but it won't equal that of Cocaine or Speed. Instead someone who was really intent on getting an energy boost greater than that which Caffeine provides, could just brew an extra strong batch of Coca Leaf tea and then consume many cups over a period of time to keep the energy level heightened.

If Heroin is physical bliss then Opium is physical peace. Plain Opium is a good alternative to the high that is Heroin and without all the chemical and excessively addictive properties that plagues Heroin. Heroin, which has been called physical bliss, creates that feeling by bringing you dangerously close to death. Opium on the other hand makes the body feel good and the mind devoid of stress without the overwhelming life numbing effect that is Heroin. Opium will also serve as a natural self-administrable painkiller for those that don't like synthetic doctor prescriptions or cannot afford them.

LSD is easily replaced by the Psychotropic Psilocybe mushrooms which create an almost 100% identical experience. They are both potentially very spiritual journeys that share all the same characteristics, bodily feelings, mental exploration and visual delights. But unlike LSD, the intensity of the experience can be varied by consuming less or more mushrooms, whereas LSD usually just comes in single, potent doses. The psychotropic Peyote cactus also fully mimics an LSD experience but varies just slightly. Any of the LSA containing psychotropic plants will mimic an LSD experience as well. DMT is also very comparable to

LSD except that it is immediately very intense and lasts for only 20 minutes.

Ecstasy is a harder experience to duplicate naturally and most people wouldn't know where to look to find its equal in the plant world. Most knowledgeable users would probably say that Psilocybe mushrooms are the closest you can get in duplicating an Ecstasy experience. This is somewhat correct except that the high created by Ecstasy does not significantly alter the mind, it only alters the body, whereas Psilocybes alter body and mind. Ecstasy is very popular because it is almost completely a body high, and although your mind is joyous and peaceful, it is not twirling the realms of your imagination and challenging your thoughts every step of the way like Psilocybe mushrooms do. The Ecstasy user can take the drug, sit back, enjoy the intense body high and focus on dancing or whatever they deem physically enjoyable without the altered mental state. Those exact qualities can be hard to find naturally, my experience leads me to a mushroom but not the Psilocybe. This psychotropic mushroom is the Amanita Muscaria, not a very common recreational mushroom at all, perhaps because it is legal and you wouldn't think of a legal psychotropic plant to be that powerful. Maybe also because when it's ingested in large quantities it can produce experiences so profound that recreational use would seem absurd. It is a powerful mushroom that quite possibility has been used religiously for longer than any other natural plant, but its use today is very rare. When prepared right and ingested in small quantities it is almost identical to the body high created by Ecstasy, with hardly any noticeable change in mind state other then peace and tranquility just like the synthetic drug Ecstasy. It is a non-addictive mushroom and yields no harm on the body or mind when used normally. In all reality though for a match that is not exact but very similar, small amounts of Psilocybe mushrooms or any LSA containing plant will be plenty sufficient in mimicking an Ecstasy experience.

It would be insane just to throw all these natural mind-altering plants out there and let people guess at which does what and how much to take. For those growing it themselves there is no need to educate them too much more about the plants, they have already done their research, that's how they learned to grow psychotropic plants in the first place. They had to do their research because with most psychotropic plants you just can't throw a seed in the ground and then get high a month later. These plants all have pretty strict growing conditions that are required, including humidity, temperature control and specific soils; they aren't as easy as growing corn. Those that don't do much growing themselves and end up buying most of their psychotropic products in the stores will be educated by the advice on the packaging. The packaging advice will be like a Surgeon Generals warning for psychotropic plants, but it needs to be more in-depth than the ones you see on alcohol and tobacco. Currently on alcohol and tobacco products there are a few warnings that rotate out, so you never really get a complete list of warnings and advise. With psychotropic plants their needs to be a full list of warnings instead of a couple that changes from pack to pack. You also want recommended dosing instructions on the packaging too.

The proper education is key in order to keep abuse to a minimum. I'm not talking about education like we have today, it is all too obvious how unsuccessful that is. We need new substance education for the youth. Education that is in-depth and effective, maybe even similar to a health class that is dedicated to what we put in our body. It would teach kids not only about psychotropic plants and synthetic drugs but also about alcohol, tobacco, Caffeine, sugar and anything else that we put in our body that has a potential for abuse. It would be a subject that is taught throughout all of one's schooling and not just during one year or one semester. Teaching adults about psychotropic plants will be done during the re-education campaign and then on the packaging of the intoxicant itself. Much of the education process will be geared towards the youth so we can prevent another generation of substance abusers like we have today. Most people you know who are addicted to drugs, alcohol, tobacco, Caffeine, sugar or just plain food are addicted to a large degree because of the failure of our current education system. They were never taught how to control their intake and unfortunately now they probably don't care about the health damages anymore because the need of fulfilling the addiction is greater than their concern over their health. Effective education can serve as a deterrent to addiction, but if someone is complacent with his or her addiction, then they have a right to indulge in it as long as they do not endanger the public while doing so. New substance education will also teach people what psychotropic plants and drugs do and what experience they create in the user. Currently if a person wants to find out what an illegal drug does and see if the intoxication appeals to them, they would have to indeed try the drug. Sometimes they end up ingesting it and are not prepared for the experience because they really never had any knowledge about the experience and the effects. Their friends may have hinted at what kind of experience to expect but that advice is often vague and does not adequately prepare them for the experience. Teaching people all about the highs and experiences that psychoactive substances produce, will equip potential users with the knowledge to decide if that particular substance appeals to them without having to blindly ingest the intoxicant first.

CHAPTER 09: DEALING WITH DRUG DISTRIBUTION AND ABUSE IN THE FREE PLANT WORLD

Making Psychotropic Plants legal is the best way to prevent people from making and distributing synthetic drugs, it has a trickle-down effect onto every single mind and body-altering substance, and effectively dissolves the underground market for them. But with the new availability of psychotropic plants there could be a greater risk of abuse, that abuse can be limited through education and adequate punishments. We'll now examine drug distribution and substance abuse in greater detail.

If these new laws are instated, which effectively legalize all psychotropic plants and allow anyone to privately manufacture and ingest any chemical drug of their choice, then it brings up obvious concerns for anyone who lacks insight into the drug culture. I am going to shed some light on these concerns. First of all, you may think that if the government allows anyone to make their own synthetic drugs and consume them privately, then we'll end up with a Meth lab on every street corner. And the manufactures will be able to sell all the Crystal Meth they want because they can now legally manufacture it under the shroud of private use. And that is a grave concern, however if you examine it with a little bit of drug insight you'll realize that when people are properly and universally educated about these dangerous substances and there exists natural legal alternatives that provide close to the same effects, then the Meth manufacturer would have no customers besides himself or his friends and family who probably wouldn't want the stuff either. So he would not even be able to give it away at this point let alone collect money for it. The bottom line is that psychotropic plants will replace synthetic drugs as long as they provide near identical effects. Since the experience from every single synthetic drug can be duplicated by a psychotropic plant or a combination of psychotropic plants, the user will gravitate to natural plants to obtain the different highs that they desire, especially when they are legal. The way to ensure that this happens is to educate the population properly on drugs, plants and the effects that they have. Let's now look at how the distribution of the major synthetic drugs will dwindle once Psychotropic Plants become legal.

With Cocaine and Heroin, traditionally it was the job of the drug cartel to obtain the plants and manufacture these drugs and then smuggle them into another country for sale. And only the drug cartel has access to the plants that make these drugs. By legalizing psychotropic plants, those who really want to ingest Cocaine and Heroin can now just make the drugs themselves a whole lot cheaper instead of supporting the drug dealers. Making these two drugs is a relatively easy process that is explained in a number of books or for free on the Internet. The required chemicals are very cheap and can easily be obtained from most chemical supply stores. But when people do attempt to make the drugs, in all likely-hood once they see the chemicals that go into the process they will no longer want to ingest the obviously harmful, chemical substance. If indeed they don't mind the unnatural substance then it is their right to ingest it in the privacy of their own home. And thankfully they will be doing so without supporting the underground drug market. Currently people who ingest these two drugs don't grow the plants themselves because cultivating the Coca Plant or Opium Poppy carries a much greater penalty and higher risk of getting caught than from just buying the end product on the street.

Crystal Meth and other synthetic drugs such as PCP are nasty chemical substances and the people who do them even know this or should know this. Use of these drugs will diminish when there are ample legal alternatives. With the proper education, people will understand how harmful these substances are and they will know how to closely duplicate the experience through safer, legal psychotropic plants. For example, the effects from energy drugs like Speed and Cocaine can be closely matched by ingesting Coca leaf tea. Ingesting alkaloids from the Coca leaf in small quantities this way, can produce effects similar to a strong coffee blend, but the more of the plant that is ingested, the more its properties of being an energizer, stimulant and anesthetic are increased. If you really wanted a distorted experience similar to PCP then you could simply ingest many cups of Coca tea and then eat some psychotropic mushrooms.

LSD and Ecstasy cannot easily be manufactured or extracted from a plant source by someone without advanced chemical knowledge. So you would think that these substances would always be distributed no matter how many plants you legalize. But the fact of the matter is that there are bunches of natural psychotropic plants that produce identical experiences. When I say identical, I mean a 95-100% exact duplication of the experience. These psychotropic plants include but are not limited to several types of mushrooms, the Peyote cactus, and the many plants that contain the chemical DMT or LSA. Therefore there is no reason to seek out one of these illegal synthetic drugs when you can get the same experience legally and naturally. For the people who do these substances, the risk of obtaining the illegal drug will not be worth it when there is a legal alternative, and the fact that it is a natural alternative makes the psychotropic plant that much more attractive. Because of the legal and natural alternatives to LSD and Ecstasy there will be no underground market for the synthetic drugs, which will put their manufactures out of business. You see, for the people who sought out hallucinating experiences LSD was a very good option because everything was illegal so it didn't matter which one you choose, LSD, Mushrooms or Peyote. LSD was only preferred because it was small, compact and easy to distribute and hide, while the other two options where big and bulky. With the legalization of Mushrooms and Peyote, LSD is no longer necessary and its distribution will diminish almost completely. LSD should however be allowed for the private chemist who mixes personal batches and gives some to friends and family, and if those acquaintances trust his recipe and will accept those types of substances then that is law abiding, assuming that no money or goods were exchanged.

The best way to deal with people who abuse mind and body altering substances is through prevention, get them before the abuse has a chance to begin. The proper education is essential along with ample government resources. This will prevent whole communities from being left behind and degrading down into havens for hopeless people, who see no better way to survive than by numbing their existence with drugs. When those two preventive methods are in widespread circulation, the majority of people who use psychotropic plants will be equipped with the knowledge and atmosphere so abuse hardly occurs. But as always there will be a small number of people who will abuse drugs and psychotropic plants no matter what. We can divide these types of substance abusers into three categories and deal with each one differently. First there will always be minors who choose to indulge in these substances and whether they consume alcohol, psychotropic plants or synthetic drugs they need a specific type of punishment. The next form of abuse is by adults who legally consume these substances but violate the law either by growing more plants then is allowed for a private grower or by exhibiting public intoxication and reckless behavior. Lastly is the group of people who distribute synthetic drugs for profit; they deserve a very harsh punishment kind of like what we have today.

The first form of abuse is with children or young people who are not of legal age to consume psychotropic plants but they do anyway and without parental administration. The only way for kids to get caught doing psychotropic plants by the police is if they are out doing them in public. So if a kid gets caught doing them in private at home then the parents will dictate the punishment, if any. But when kids ingest the plants or show signs of intoxication in public or at school, it is the police who will be dealing with them. Expelling a young person from school is not the most appropriate answer, which is what often happens today after only one Marijuana offense. Instead you should levy fines against the parents and also require community service on the part of the child. So for the first intoxication offense maybe something like $150 fine for the parents and 16 hours of community service that the child will work off during a weekend. If the child continues to get caught ingesting psychotropic plants then the fines and amount of community service should double every time. Making it 16 hours for the first offense, 30 hours for the 2nd offense and 60 hours for an additional one. It is only then that additional offenses would permit harsher punishments such as stays in juvenile detention. The public service workload would not exceed the number of hours allowed for a child to work during a school week, but conveniently many accumulated hours can easily be worked off during the summer months, a dreaded punishment for school youths on vacation. Fines for parents could range up to $500 after several occurrences. For the most part though, any kid that gets forced into working a couple of shifts at a public service facility will think long and hard before they try to get high in public again. All children through their drug education will be taught that kids getting high in public is against the law and it is only allowed in private or in a religious institution with parental supervision, and kids who disobey that law may incur not only fines for the family but also community service labor hours payable by them, the offending youth. It is a very effective intoxication deterrent because only requiring the parents to pay a fine has minimal affect on the child, but if you force the kid to give up their free time to work some boring public service job then it becomes an effective punishment and an adequate deterrent.

Secondly there is the abuse that stems from adults; this type of abuse has a few different levels such as growing more psychotropic plants than is allowed for private use and those that drive a vehicle while intoxicated or exhibit public intoxication. It is okay for a person to grow a large amount of psychotropic plants on their private property, even an amount that exceeds the private limit as long as they have secured the proper license beforehand. Obtaining that license would simply require a trip to the appropriate government licensing office and explaining your need to grow more psychotropic plants, and if approved you pay the fee and obtain the license. That way when a police officer drives by your yard someday and sees your garden of 100+ Opium Poppy flowers all he has to do is look up the residence in his computer and see that the owner and property have the license to grow such an amount. The officer doesn't even have to bother you to see that you're registered with the state. The reason you need the license is because you are a private citizen who wishes to grow a commercial amount of psychotropic plants and you must be registered to do that so the government knows your reasons and that you aren't trying to make a profit from the plants or drugs that you may produce. Failing to have the license would constitute fines and punishment. If you have a few more plants over what is allowed then only a warning may be issued but if you have a substantial amount over the limit, then it can only be assumed that you are participating in underground activity and large fines may be levied as well as community service or jail time if it is found to be a large unlicensed growing operation. People who consume psychotropic plants or homemade drugs and exhibit reckless behavior should be punished adequately. The method for determining what substance someone has taken and when will be the saliva test. Although in its infancy right now with accuracy and use, the saliva test has the potential with a little more research and development to be an extremely accurate roadside substance test. Saliva tests aren't very good at determining whether someone did a psychoactive substance within the last couple of days but they are useful in finding out if someone did one in the last couple of hours, which is really all that is needed to know. It doesn't matter if someone did a psychotropic plant or drug yesterday or the day before, we need to know if they've done one recently before they started driving a vehicle. If a cop pulls someone over and suspects that they might be on something, he can then just swab their mouth run the saliva through an analyzer and know roughly the amount of a substance they ingested and how long ago they did it. These tests need to be developed a little further so they are extremely accurate; arresting someone for driving six hours after ingesting Marijuana is not an appropriate law enforcement practice. So the tests need to be accurate enough to determine the time of ingestion. Salvia tests have the potential to accomplish this successfully. Now when someone is busted for driving under the influence of a psychoactive substance and it is determined that they recently consumed the substance, then they should be treated no differently than a drunk driver. Drunk and drugged driving is a serious problem in today's society, it takes thousands of lives every year. But if you think in futuristic terms, you may eventually see an end to the intoxicated driver problem. It is too early for anyone to give an accurate time frame but it is becoming more apparent that with the progression of technology, we will eventually have automatic transportation. They may be in the form of self-driving cars or some sort of small personal flying craft guided by Global Positioning Satellites. The infancy of these technologies already exist and so it gives some hope in having a society free from intoxicated drivers someday, even if it is a couple of generations away. For those people who are intoxicated in public, they should be taken to a holding cell and allowed to detoxify for certain period of time. Depending on what substance was consumed the duration that they are held for will differ. If people consume a substance that usually has lasting effects for six hours or more like Heroin, Opium, Mushrooms and Peyote then they should be placed in the holding cell for 12 hours or so and when they are released they must pay some fines. For less intoxicating substance such as Marijuana, a record of their name should be taken and a fine issued.

Lastly are those who distribute synthetic drugs for profit, these are really any distributors or manufactures who are in the business of selling illegal synthetic drugs. And although we have already established that there won't be much of a market for these types of substances once Psychotropic Plants become legal, there needs to be adequate punishment so as to deter or punish those who choose to participate in this activity. What needs to happen is that every case should be looked at individually, there should be no mandatory minimums and the punishment shouldn't be 20 years like it is today. It should be more like 3-5 years for distributing substantial quantities of synthetic drugs. The only drug dealers who should serve hard time are those who are involved in distributing very large quantities. If a small-time drug dealer is a non-violent offender and has no other criminal history other than the minor drug-related offense, they should not just be shipped away to prison for several years. Instead they should enter a house arrest program where they can do regular community service and be assigned a job by their probation officer. Each case should be examined individually because drug distributors sell drugs for different reasons. Obviously they do it for money but leniency needs to be shown if the dealer is found to be selling drugs to support his family or if the dealer is an addict. Packing these types of people into prison only causes further havoc to the individual and to their family, plus it wastes more taxpayers' money because these people are not given any appropriate options that help them escape the life, so they usually end up back in jail. If one person is trying to provide for themselves and their three kids but cannot do so without selling drugs, then the government needs to provide aid to people in these types of poverty situations. Once the government is no longer broke from waging a senseless Drug War, they will have the resources to help these families. On the other hand if an individual is only supporting him or herself and is more than able to do so but chooses to sell drugs instead, then they should be susceptible to a harsher punishment.

As you can see, the individual drug dealer will become an almost extinct operator in society once psychotropic plants take hold, but when they do get caught it is irresponsible to punish drug dealers in a way that gives them no alternatives to get out of the lifestyle. So the proper punishments are a required precondition, therefore they should be devised thoughtfully. When dealing with substance abuse, education is the number one deterrent and we have seen what bad education gets us, very little deterring from harmful substances.

CHAPTER 10: THE ROADMAP

The problem with the legalization effort today is that there are too many organizations chasing different ideals. They are all spending their time and money on different paths to ease the Drug War. Some pursue the legalization of Marijuana while others just work for decriminalized Marijuana or medical prescription Marijuana only. Then there are those who either want all drug laws reformed plus Marijuana legalized, or all drug laws reformed without Marijuana legalized. The opinions among all these different drug policy reform groups are extremely varied, each one proposing their own corrections for the War on Drugs, and all of them possessing no real unity that is bonded together by a common greater goal. And although the larger organizations have the resources to get some drug law reforms passed, the bills themselves have little over all impact and carry no real long-term direction. This dividing and spreading of funds, time, and energy is not going to lead to any major changes in drug legislation. There needs to be a consensus and one greater goal or purpose established that everyone is fully dedicated to; all legalization groups need to combine into one centralized effort and share in the direction to move that aim ahead. A single treasury needs to be established to collect all donations; you can't continue to have different people donating to different legalization causes. All the money needs to go to one place, and that money needs to be saved and built up for a massive re-education program for the public, which will eventually lead up to the public voting on the new drug-law proposals.

Making psychotropic plants legal encompasses every objective that today's legalization and decriminalization groups could ever hope to achieve, but it also still manages to maintain many of the modern-day restraints on harmful synthetic drugs and their distribution. This idea has the potential to be the solution to the War on Drugs and if all the drug-law reform groups can agree that the legalization of psychotropic plants is the greater common goal and combine forces for that sole achievement, then the new drug law is very obtainable. How you get to that end result of voter approval on the freeing of plants will take a lot of hard work and campaigning plus a significant amount of money, but once all the information and scenarios are laid out to the undecided voter, they will understand how the legalization of psychotropic plants will dissolve the War on Drugs and vote in favor. It is only after the majority of Americans vote in favor to legalize psychotropic plants, that we can then demand the legislative branch of government to form the accompanying laws. The legislative branch of government will never fix the Drug War on its own, the people will have to decide what drug laws they want and then demand our elected officials pass them into law.

Once the common goal of legalizing all plants is accepted by the majority of drug law reform groups, there needs to be a full establishment of communications and direction between them. Possibly one large group or alliance needs to take the lead or a new organization could be established to direct and lead the overall movement. The head group needs to pull resources and talent from all the little groups, fill top positions with the best people from the many different reform groups. There needs to be a lot of great minds working together on this effort, but they all need to be on the same page with one goal, the legalization of all plants. When the head alliance is built it will have two main objectives to accomplish. It will need to devise, discuss and eventually write pertinent drug legislation for the people to vote on, while also constructing and executing a widespread public education campaign.

Collecting money for the effort is the easy part but it needs to be hoarded away and not spent for years until the campaign begins. It will take a lot of money and it will be just as if you're pushing a presidential candidate during an election year. With two differences, first the campaign will begin more than four years before the election and second, it's not a person you're trying to get the public acquainted with and then elected, it is an idea. The idea being the legalization of all plants and it will take television ads in every state, magazine and newspaper ads, public events as well as some educational films for the public to be able to comprehend the subject and not fear it. There needs to be a lot of brainstorming in order to find the best methods to get the ideas across to the voters. Realistically it may take over four years to raise enough money for the campaign and then another four years of actually implementing the re-education campaign before it is successful enough to get a majority vote. All the people who know absolutely nothing about drugs, what they are and where they come from, will be properly educated during the public campaign so that if legalized, everyone will have a good foundation so that if they do choose to ingest these substances they will be able to do so responsibly. After the campaign is over education will continue in school for the young people, so that when they are of age they will already be aware of the proper way to ingest mind and body altering substances. There needs to be a lot of research done on the many aspects of plant legalization, including how much money it could possibly free up for the betterment of society. Getting Americans to favor this idea will take a considerable amount of work, much more work than would be required in some European countries. In fact some other countries may invoke the plan in their country long before the campaign in America even begins, if that happens then it will serve as an example for the U.S. and make the campaign that much easier. It is really up to America to legalize plants before the rest of the world can collectively sigh and ease up on their own plant restrictions because the US is the main propulsion of the Drug War. Maybe it's because we're the biggest consumers of mind and body altering substances.

There are several groups that are currently making some progress on drug law reform but it is minimal. The biggest campaign right now is for the medicinal use of Marijuana and it has made strides compared to a decade ago, but it is still far from being fully realized. The campaign for medicinal Marijuana will have to be canceled in order for the legalization of all plants to have a chance in the near future. The campaign for medicinal Marijuana spends the majority of drug law reform funds. That campaign will have to end and those resources will have to be rededicated to the legalization of all psychotropic plants since they both effectively provide the same outcome. There is only one goal in this new philosophy on drug law reform but it encompasses all the objectives set out by other drug policy reform organizations.

All the money saved from waging the War on Drugs, plus the additional taxes created from people legitimately buying psychotropic plants will bring in an enormous amount of money for the government. And with all the reckless spending by the government, dividing the Drug War and making plants profitable will be a very attractive idea to most people because it could very easily wipe out the national deficit and get the economy booming as we head into the new future. Of course psychotropic plant use will increase but it will also simultaneously and substantially decrease the synthetic drug market. The proper public education will prevent people from abusing psychotropic plants and the proper laws will punish those who do.

Chapter 11: Conclusion

The world cannot move ahead until the Drug War is solved. It is only then that we can really devote full time and resources to helping the humanitarian crises that affect this planet today. On the local level drug distribution spurs crime and violence but globally it funds international terrorism and gives many corrupt people unlimited money and power. It is quite possible that if we could end the Drug War it could be the solution of this first quandary that could eventually lead to the end of most worldwide suffering. By ending the Drug War you free up a lot of money as well as acquire more money from psychotropic plant taxation. This subsequently leads to a substantial diminishing of funds for the international terrorist groups and although they will still obtain some money from donations by wealthy and radical religious people, it will drastically cut into their finances. Making that global problem very manageable and possibly even conquerable. So then you can free up even more money and resources for the government that can then be invested in things like fighting poverty worldwide or ending the AIDS problem in Africa. It would also enable international peacekeepers to fight off guerrilla warfare and militias much more effectively, plus give the world more resources to fight child prostitution and other intolerable crimes of humanity. Once these global issues get solved we can then use all the excess resources and money to advance technology and medicine and help get the planet and environment back to a healthy condition that will support modern life for the long term. Having plenty of new resources could easily end oil dependency too. It is the cessation of the Drug War that could very well be the first step in ending the global problems that currently plague human existence. And we should seek to end the Drug War because it revolves around what an individual chooses to put in his or her own body, that is a choice for the person to be making and not society.

Of course if someone accepts a job as an athlete they should not be allowed to use certain performance enhancing substances that would give them an unfair competitive edge. Players accept this agreement when they sign their contract, effectively paying them not to put certain substances in their body. Athletes who do ingest soft plants like Marijuana should not be penalized if they are also allowed to ingest alcohol at times during the season or in the off-season. That all makes sense for professional athletes. But why do we prohibit the public from putting certain substances in their body? Why haven't we been able to devise adequate laws that allow people to ingest what they want while also protecting society against harm? Those are two questions I am not going to attempt to answer. What I will say though, is that throughout history it has always been the societal game of cops and robbers, not cops and druggies. It was the good guys verses the bad guys, the bad guys being the murders, the robbers, the muggers or other people who willfully commit acts of crime and violence. It has only been recently augmented to include people who ingest euphoric substances. Now cops waste their time persecuting substance users while drug-related crime makes their jobs even more dangerous. We need to solve the Drug War through legislation so that law enforcement can refocus their attention back on the issues that are really detrimental to society.

If we do not solve the Drug War now, then what will happen when technology advances and new synthetic recreational drugs are developed and circulated? The War on Drugs will have to expand and the funds and resources that are already being dedicated will have to increase also. But it is painfully obvious that we cannot dedicate any more funds to fighting the Drug War, taking more money from the budget would drastically affect the governments other responsibilities. We cannot successfully fight the Drug War as it is and if new, profitable synthetic drugs where to ever reach the market then drug culture, crime and corruption would grow beyond control overwhelming the world even more then it does today. That is why we must allow for the existence of some substances that make people high. There is no better option than to absolve psychotropic plants from the Drug War. Doing so would not only abolish our current underground drug market but would also prevent any new synthetic drugs from gaining widespread appeal because people will have readily available legal alternatives. The inventing of new and advanced synthetic drugs will eventually occur but if they are developed before the Drug War is abolished then they will become extremely profitable. Adding these new psychoactive drugs to an already uncontrollable war that we have on the current drugs and psychotropic plants, will definitely exhaust all resources possibly leading to many worldwide catastrophes. But on the other hand if new and advanced synthetic drugs are invented after the Drug War is abolished, then they will only exist among a small private class who develops them exclusively for friends, family and personal use. That's because making synthetic drugs is not like splitting atoms, it is a relatively easy chemical process that anyone could duplicate, the only requirement is a working knowledge of chemistry but even that can be self taught through various books and other resources. Therefore new and advanced synthetic drugs will have a very minimal profitability because anyone could follow the recipe and make these drugs, so if a market for a new synthetic drug developed, then competition would quickly bring the price down making its distribution almost immediately unprofitable. The new drug would only be profitable if the recipe was kept a secret, but that is unlikely because chemical analysis can tell you what is in the substance and then with the Internet, books and widespread circulation of knowledge, all types of recipes quickly get distributed for free. Today people cannot easily manufacture and sell their own drugs because very few people have access to either the plants that make Heroin, Cocaine and Marijuana, or the chemicals that make LSD, MDMA and Speed. As you can imagine, if everyone had access to those precursors then profitable distribution wouldn't exist.

Drug use itself or the act of getting high has an almost negligible effect on society. It is undeniably the crime, corruption, and violence, which in turn gets combated with many hundreds of billions of dollars each year netting near zero results that is most harmful. Even a junkie who's high all day couldn't inflict more harm on society than when the drugs they seek were illegal and extremely expensive. It may seem that if psychotropic plants were legal and widespread then an increasing number of people would develop into junkies, who would then become bums on the street that sit around all day and get high. That would make society slowly start to decay because no one would want to work anymore. But you see if our society was that vulnerable then alcohol would of done it a long time ago. Plus we have always had good access to psychotropic plants and drugs, supply has never been an issue especially for the youth and there never has been anything close to an enormous population of junkies. The fact is that the number of drug abusers we have today will stay the same even when we legalize plants, but the number of responsible users will go up. The percentage of people that use psychotropic plants in some form or another may after 50 years or so top 50%. But a lot of people will use them for medicine or therapy. It may even become common for someone to have Coca tea in their kitchen or a little Opium in their first aid kit. Plus quite possibly anyone who indulged in alcohol before psychotropic plants were made legal has the potential to use plants to obtain a natural high. That would indeed make for a large population of plant users. The number of responsible psychotropic plant users is meaningless, it doesn't matter how many there are. What holds significance is the number of abusers that co-populate the world with everyone else. Abuse can be held to a minimum because psychotropic plants are less prone to abuse than synthetic drugs and once plants take over the synthetic drug market, drug use and abuse will decrease. The fact is that no plants are more harmful than alcohol when abused and only Opium is close to being equal with alcohol in terms of possible abuse. But Opium will never have the widespread appeal that alcohol has because the high is only attractive to a small minority of people. Most people will not obtain recreational pleasure from the ingestion of Opium because the experience is just too sedating for them to enjoy. And for the small number of people who use Opium, only a tiny fraction of them will turn it into Heroin. This handful of possible Heroin users represent the type of people who would seek out the drug anyway. So whether it's illegal, or legal for private use, the junkie population will barely increase. The problems from drug abuse have never been equal to the havoc created by the Drug War, and even with limited resources we have still managed to keep public drug abuse at a minimum. If we had more money and resources then law enforcement would be even better equipped to keep abuse down, even if the number of abusers slightly increases with the new availability of intoxicating substances.

All in all, in a modern and free plant society, individuals will be disparaged if they come off as not having control of their plants or drugs because any abuse will be evident to others. If you want to be a respectable businessperson but have an Opium addiction and people notice that, then you can't expect to get as good of a job or regular promotions. Just with alcoholics, professional businesses do not want people who have uncontrollable substance problems. It affects their job in many negative ways. Currently many addicts waste their life a way with their addiction while maintaining low-level jobs. These are often physical labor jobs and although not everyone in the working class is an addict, the demanding nature of the job makes different substances very appealing. Pain relieving substances such as alcohol, Opiates and Marijuana are often ingested after a long hard day. And while on the job a person may use high-energy substances such as Cocaine, Speed, Caffeine or Coca tea. No matter what the level of addiction, they can maintain it if that is their desire. Unfortunately the more addicts there are in a community, the greater that community is at risk for deteriorating. That is where localized taxes come in, as with alcohol the local government will collect a portion of psychotropic plant taxes. And just like alcoholics most addicts will buy their substance of choice in the stores instead of making it or growing it themselves. If someone is too lazy or hopeless to prevent their own addiction then they likewise will be too lazy or hopeless to make the intoxicant themselves. You just don't see alcoholics brewing their own Beer or Wine to feed their addiction, they almost always buy it in the stores forcing them to pay taxes on the substance. So Opium addicts will also be more inclined to buy it instead of grow it. Well the more addicts there are in a community, then the more resources that community will have available to deal with the problem. There will be more resources to indeed help addicts with their problem but the taxes will also allow a high community living standard to be upheld. More money will allow for the city to be kept clean of litter and debris while also keeping parks and public areas maintained. It will also provide law enforcement with the staff and resources to keep addicts off the streets. Plus the tax money would assure that the local schools are well maintained and their programs are effective and educational, which would prevent more people from becoming addicts. If someone does have a neighbor who grows a rather large amount of Opium Poppies and exhibits an addiction to Opium, then it would be nice of them to get to know the grower and possibly see if they're interested in recovery. Whether it's Opium, alcohol or Nicotine that someone is addicted to, those close to the addict should voice their persuasion to quit. If the abuse is extensive in someone's life then friends and family would also have the option of notifying the local rehab center so that they can make a free visit. But a private drug or plant addiction is legally acceptable and addicts who get intoxicated at home should not be arrested. At least this way addicts can positively contribute to their community through taxes. These taxes should always be high on psychotropic plants and we have established how that can be done. It is equally important however that we raise the taxes on legal psychoactive substances. Alcohol taxes should be raised once psychotropic plants are legalized and so should the taxes on tobacco products. Caffeine products should also have a tax that is recoverable for the government. Especially bulk Caffeine products like large cans of coffee and Caffeine pills. If it is a legal psychoactive substance that has any addiction possibility whatsoever, then it should be highly taxed by the government. And if you choose to commercially purchase your addiction, then the government will recover an adequate amount of money allowing them to protect society against the abuse of intoxicants, and maintain an effective educational program that teaches the youth and helps prevent more substance addiction.

The War on Drugs in its current state could continue indefinitely with very little success. Every year the price tag for America alone is equal to the cost of maintaining a moderate sized military war. And every year we lose that war because there are only minuscule changes in the supply and demand of drugs. America is a super power with the most advanced military on the planet and it has won many wars in the past and helped win many wars. But the Drug War is one that it will never win. It is a war that has been fought continuously for over 100 years and in the last 30 years it has been intensified to the extreme, but the results nevertheless always fail to materialize. Fundamentally it is flawed in every way. Even drug education has been propelled into an ineffective program designed to propagate exaggerations, instead of equipping the youth with the required knowledge so that they can make good decisions regarding psychoactive substances. The War on Drugs is not fought on foreign soil against other people, it is a war against its own people on its own land. Aggressively going after drug distributors and drug crime helps protect society, but there wouldn't be any drug distributors or drug-related crime in the first place if people were allowed to grow, make and eat psychoactive substances in the privacy of their own homes.

As long as psychotropic plants are banned synthetic drugs will steadily begin to take over the market. That is because they are small, compact and highly profitable whereas psychotropic plants are bulky, less profitable and a lot harder to conceal and distribute. In some local drug markets you can really only get synthetic drugs or Marijuana. For some people who want a major buzz, their only option is a synthetic substance because that is all that is available and so they buy and ingest synthetic drugs. Alternative psychotropic plants are slowly being squeezed off the drug market. Anyone who has experience buying illegal substances from the underground drug market knows how much easier it is to get synthetic drugs. For the hallucinogen user, they are almost always able to obtain LSD, but psychotropic mushrooms are rare and only circulate every once in a while. Plain Opium almost never makes its rounds in the American drug market. It is very easy to get Heroin but it is almost impossible for the average person to obtain Opium. Cocaine and Speed are also popular and easy to obtain because the Coca Plant itself is just not available to the common person. Marijuana has already been bred into a more potent form, which makes smaller amounts cost more so distributors can make the same profits while distributing less. But pretty soon even Marijuana may begin appearing in synthetic forms that are easier to distribute, such as liquid THC that people put on a legal smoking herb or tobacco. Synthetic THC pills could also become popular. The distribution of Hashish isn't more widespread because it is too inefficient to make, but if someone found an easy way to make synthetic THC then it could very likely become a new widespread drug. If the current Drug War is maintained then all illegal substances will eventually gravitate to forms that are much more concealable, making them easier to distribute. In almost all occurrences they become compact, potent synthetic substances.

The legalization of all psychotropic plants will end the Drug War. It will take the plants away from the drug makers and put them in the hands of the people who use them. The chain of dealers and countless middlemen who induce violence and crime will no longer exist. The rich, powerful and corrupt drug lords will fade into the past. The inner cities that are over run by drugs and crime will revitalize and become healthy environments. Even junkies will now be able to afford their junk instead of robbing and mugging innocent people for money. And at last America will finally have the money and resources that are needed to develop and execute an effective educational program that prevents abuse by accurately teaching about psychoactive substances and their effects. It should be very apparent now that we need to make effective policy changes regarding the War on Drugs. Small reforms like decriminalization or mandatory rehabilitation is not nearly enough. Instead of slightly altering the War on Drugs, let's take the opportunity to end the war forever and put the resources to good use. In the end it doesn't really matter if psychotropic plants are made commercially available or if we allow the existence of public facilities where people can get high. What will really have an impact on the War on Drugs is if we allow a person to grow their own psychotropic plants and ingest what they want in private. It is amazing that a few plants could have such a major impact on the world and as we've seen banning them has led to a major global problem. If legalizing a few plants is all it would take to responsibly end the global War on Drugs and close that chapter in our history, then we should expediently look into that option. Because really all we are talking about is a couple of plants, a few mushrooms, a cactus and a flower, hardly anything worth wagging a worldwide war against.

www.ingramcontent.com/pod-product-compliance
Lightning Source LLC
Chambersburg PA
CBHW061244280526
45784CB00002B/628